HELP!
I'M A BABY BOOMER

P9-CQD-000

HELP!
I'M A BABY BOOMER

HANS
FINZEL

VICTOR BOOKS®
A DIVISION OF SCRIPTURE PRESS PUBLICATIONS INC.
USA CANADA ENGLAND

Other Victor Books by Hans Finzel
Unlocking the Scriptures
Opening the Book

Unless otherwise noted, Scripture quotations are from the *Holy Bible, New International Version,* © 1973, 1978, 1984, International Bible Society. Used by permission of Zondervan Bible Publishers. Quotations marked NASB are from the *New American Standard Bible,* © the Lockman Foundation 1960, 1962, 1963, 1968, 1971, 1972, 1973, 1975, 1977.

Recommended Dewey Decimal Classification: 248.7

Suggested Subject Heading: PERSONAL CHRISTIANITY: BABY BOOMERS

Library of Congress Catalog Card Number: 88-62868

ISBN: 0-89693-632-5

© 1989 by SP Publications, Inc. All rights reserved. Printed in the United States of America. No part of this book may be used or reproduced in any manner whatsoever without written permission except in the case of brief quotations in critical articles and reviews. For information, address Victor Books, Wheaton, IL 60187.

Contents

92501

This book is dedicated to two of my closest friends, one on each side of the Atlantic:

Mike Wilson & Craig Weaver

"A friend loves at all times,
and a brother is born for adversity."
—Proverbs 17:17

Acknowledgments

I am indebted to my dear wife, Donna, for her patience and servant spirit during the birth of this book, which, unfortunately, coincided with the birth of our twins. For the excellent discussion questions, I thank my brother of encouragement, Craig Weaver. I also very much appreciate Scott Last for his insightful chapter on "Singlehood." Of course my editor, Afton Rorvik, needs heaps of credit. And, finally, I thank Hewlett-Packard for creating my laptop computer without which I never would have attempted or completed this project on the run.

Introduction

This is a book by and about baby boomers. In case you didn't notice, the generation born between 1946 and 1964 is slowly taking over our country and our churches, and *that* makes them worth looking at in a new light. A fad has been defined as "something that goes in one era and out the other." You'll soon see that tracking baby boomers is not a fad because our sheer size makes us a force and an influence in American society that must continually be reckoned with. Our influence is only gaining ground across our land—we are fast becoming the new "grown ups"—a massive new power bloc in America with very opinionated views about almost everything.

Consider this: the U.S. Census Bureau estimates that *76 million* people were born in the U.S. between 1946 and 1964. Add to that number all of the children boomers have had (we are on the verge of what I call a *boomer boom*), and you arrive at a total of at least 130 million people—*half of the population of the United States!* Boomers are indeed the largest generation ever seen in this country, and all projections indicate that these numbers will not be matched again in the lifetime of anyone reading this book.

No longer just making noise on the sidelines, boomers are taking charge of the corporations, factories, organizations, schools, and churches of our land. With this positioning comes *influence,* the power to change the way things are viewed and done. In short, baby boomers are taking over and running America!

I am a card-carrying baby boomer, born in 1951 to German parents in Huntsville, Alabama. I arrived in the world squarely in the bulge of the early boom years. During the 60s I became a *hippie* and a *yippie*, deeply involved in the drug counterculture and the student riots on my college campus, the University of Alabama. Many of us dropped out of the path our parents had planned for us, rejecting en masse the world their generation was handing us on a not-so-silver platter. I guess we realized later that our solutions to the ills of this world weren't much better than theirs, but at least we tried to make a difference as a generation.

At every turn of my life, even now as I approach the benchmark 40, my consciousness of who I am always seems to be influenced by certain baby-boomer values. We seem to have a consciousness as a generation that holds us together like glue—values, beliefs, and attitudes unique to us.

We need to understand ourselves better. We need to understand where the battles are being fought over the values of this generation. Anyone who is a baby boomer and also committed to a lifestyle of obedience to Jesus Christ needs to recognize some of the unique pressures that our generation puts on us, forcing us at times to shout, "Help! I'm a baby boomer."

In this journey through a generation, we will look at *who* the baby boomers really are, *what* they believe (unique value systems), and *how* Christian boomers can cope with the unique pressures of their generation. We will propose some alternative lifestyle values for Christian boomers who want to do more than survive, who want to impact their generation for Christ. At the end of each chapter, I've included questions which will help you think through important issues. The questions may also be used for group study.

The goal of this book is to crawl inside the head of the baby boomer to understand what makes this generation tick and the unique traits and values that have welded our generation together in strange ways. To understand our roots is to understand our values. But we really only *start* there. Understanding must lead to action. We must *impact the biggest generation America has ever seen.* We will have to use different methods and different approaches—even a new language—because each generation has its own set of values and perspectives, like a new culture in a foreign land.

No one is sure how many baby boomers are also believers—followers of Jesus Christ committed to making a difference in their world. The numbers are unimportant. What is important is their influence. One of the basic questions this book asks is, *"Who is influencing whom?"* What effect is the general value system and lifestyle of baby boomers having on Christians trying to live a Christ-honoring life? And vice versa, what impact are we believing boomers having on our fellow generation? That last question is the critical issue of this book.

In writing this book, I have studied contemporary literature in books and periodicals about our baby-boom generation to discover what people are saying about us and the times in which we live. The collective consciousness of our generation comes through loud and clear, in countless books, movies, TV shows, and newspaper and magazine articles. I have tried to summarize and present that consciousness—our generational values—and then run them through my own biblical convictions as a believing boomer. I trust the results will be as enlightening for you as they have been for me.

Hans Finzel
January 1989
Garden Grove, California

1

A Fresh Look at the Baby-Boom Bulge

"By 1990, those aged 25 to 44 will control 44% of all households and 55% of consumer spending and be a majority of the electorate."

U.S. News & World Report

Me, turning 40? Is it really possible?

One greeting card maker—yet another industry that caters to the consumer appetite of baby boomers—has come out with a whole new line of cards just for those of us turning 40.

This new line of birthday cards, called "Over the Hill" cards, really knows how to rub it in. The cover of one reads, *"Now that you're over the hill, you've got it all. . . ."* Inside the card descriptive words complete the thought: *". . . bulges, sags, wrinkles, flab, back pain, hearing loss, flat feet and fatigue."* Oh, the woes of aging boomers!

Card makers can stand to make some serious cash on these cards. Over the next 18 years around 4 million Americans will turn 40 each year.

Because it is such a large group of the U.S. population, the baby-boom generation has a lot of clout in society and

13

business, including the greeting card industry.

Who are these people?

This book answers that question.

What Caused the Boom Anyway?

Why did our parents all of a sudden start having babies? The answer is tied to what was happening to our country in the mid-1940s: World War II. Economic hard times, the gloom of war, and the separation of most women from their husbands had kept young couples, our parents, from having babies. It's hard to make babies when you're separated by oceans!

In Europe, where my parents spent the war, World War II had left behind such devastation that it would be another five years before the inhabitants felt settled enough to devote themselves to serious baby-making. But those countries that had not become battlegrounds, the United States, Canada, Australia, and New Zealand, experienced an immediate baby boom.

Many lives were lost during the war, but Americans came out of the war as winners with the worldwide reputation as the liberators of the oppressed. America was the primary power behind the cause of freedom. It was a time to be proud. It was a time to feel good about the future. It was time to settle down and raise a family. Americans were so confident about the future and determined to make up for lost time that the birthrate in 1947 was higher than at any time since the post World War I baby boom of 1921.

Statistics of an Emerging Generation

There is no question about it—the end of World War II brought on the baby boom. In May of 1946, *nine months after V-J Day*, there were an unprecedented 233,452 births in one month in the U.S. By the year's end, an all-time U.S. record (up to that point) of *3.4 million babies* had been born—the biggest baby boom in U.S. history had begun. By the end of 1949, that total was brought up to 14.5 million. By 1954, our parents were producing 4 million babies every year. A new kind of invasion was taking place in America!

It was not until 1964, when the first boomers started getting married, that the birthrate began to fall below the 4 million mark. The birthrate in those years of 1946 to 1964 averaged 25 percent per 1,000 population, meaning that 250 women out of every 1,000 were having babies. Now, 3.5 million babies are born in the U.S. each year, but we have a much larger population and the rate is only 15 percent per 1,000, or 150 women out of every 1,000 having a child in a given year (Johnson 1988:790).

In March of 1986, *U.S. News & World Report* celebrated the birthday of our generation with a special issue devoted to looking at baby boomers reaching mid-life. The issue was written to celebrate the fortieth birthday of the first crop of baby boomers. In the feature article entitled "You've Come a Long Way Baby Boomers—When a Generation Turns Forty," the author describes boomers in this way:

> As infants, they made diaper industry revenues soar more than 50% by 1957. As children, they swelled school enrollment by two thirds. (Have you noticed how many schools are now closed in your neighborhood?) As adults, they created such job competition that between 1973 and 1980 medium income for young men fell 17%.
>
> By 1990, those aged 25 to 44 will control 44% of all households and 55% of consumer spending and be a majority of the electorate (Rosellini 1986:60).

Baby boomers are the best educated 40-year-olds in American history, with an average of 12.9 years of formal schooling. More than 84 percent of us have completed high school, and almost half of us have finished a year of college. A total of 25.1 percent have attended four or more years of college (Rosellini 1986:61).

At age 40, boomers are twice as likely to have been through a divorce as their counterparts living in 1947 when the boom began. About 80 percent of male boomers are married, and 77 percent of the females are married. Many of these marriages are remarriages, and the children of baby boomers today have some rather interesting networking going on as they try to stay in touch with their natural fathers and mothers.

Two Waves of Baby Boomers

The official demographers of the U.S. government bracket the baby-boom generation between 1946 (the first full postwar year in which birthrates surged) and 1964 (after which the birthrate fell). Now, of course, those of you like my older brother Peter, born in 1945, just before the official boom began, should not feel excluded. For all practical purposes, you're boomers too, by virtue of rubbing shoulders with the giant generation all your lives.

People born in the late 1940s obviously view life differently than people born in the early 1960s. Most experts who write about the boomer generation view 1957, the peak year of the boom, as the watershed year between two groups of baby boomers.

The Early Boomers. The half of our generation born in or before 1957 was the most influenced by the turbulent '60s. It was this group, of which I am a part, that was radically and permanently altered by the events and social movements of the '60s and early '70s. It is this group that is now turning 40 and making its values felt across our land.

This early wave of boomers experienced the assassination of John F. Kennedy. We all remember where we were and how we felt on that November day in 1963. This was perhaps the first and most stirring political memory for early baby boomers, but the event meant little to the second wave of boomers, barely out of diapers on November 22, 1963.

Other events, like the moon landing and Woodstock in the summer of 1969, also had a powerful impact on this budding generation of early boomers. Of course, the Vietnam War was fought during the '60s and early '70s. Fifty-eight thousand soldiers, mostly baby boomers, gave their lives in this unpopular war. Three hundred thousand came home wounded, and 75,000 were permanently disabled in this war that sparked our rebellion as a generation (Simon 1988:3). Then Watergate in the early '70s completed our social fermentation as we sought a better way to run our country. These powerful forces on the political and social scenes in the '60s and early '70s made lasting impressions on the early wave of baby boomers, impressions that in turn shaped the values of a generation.

The Late Boomers. The triumphs and tragedies of the early boomers were merely pages from newly published history books to their younger siblings born after 1957. Perhaps the difference between the two groups is best put by Landon Jones, executive editor of *Money Magazine,* who has written what many feel to be the definitive work on the baby boomers. He says:

> The older half of the generation was the most idealistic and the most easily disappointed. They're what people think of as baby boomers.
>
> The second half had diminished expectations. They were more realistic. They looked ahead and saw the world was crowded. They didn't think life would be handed to them on a silver platter. As for their cultural experiences, the older half was more euphoric. They were the youth society, the protesters. They had the sense that youth could take over the world, that rock and roll would bind us. The younger half had no charge. For them, rock and roll is taken for granted, and youth is something you had to pass through (Ingrassia 1986:14).

As we'll see in later chapters, economic differences between the two groups are profound. The earlier group got the better treatment in their childhood, better educations in college, and the pick of jobs while there was still an abundance to choose from. Then came the 1970s when this late boomer group hit the job market and found it glutted with the early boomers.

It is this group of late boomers that is probably thought of as the "Me Generation," lacking a deeply developed social consciousness and seeking the American dream full steam ahead.

Ironically, it is the early boomers that began with such anti-materialistic zeal and ended up with all the "goodies" of affluence in the 1980s. The late boomers, focused on finding the good life right out of college, have had a very hard time reaching it. Whereas the early group could afford to buy houses when houses were still within reach, many of the later group have been shut out by skyrocketing prices unless they join the crowd of two-income families.

Oh, How We Love Labels!

The entire baby-boom generation is unique in a number of ways. It is the first generation to grow up with the threat of nuclear war, television, space exploration, the Pill, and LSD. It is a generation born right after the *good war* and thrown into the middle of what most felt was a very *bad war*.

We are also unique because we have become the most labeled generation in U.S. history. We have been dubbed the:

- **Baby boomers**
- **TV generation**
- **Love generation**
- **Now generation**

- **Spock generation**
- **Vietnam generation**
- **Me generation**
- **Pepsi generation**

Then there are more labels for subgroups within our generation. Consider the following:

- **the drug culture**—drug-using baby boomers who formed their own society within society in the 1960s and early 1970s.

- **the counterculture**—a generic grouping of the campus activists and hippie types of the 1960s.

- **flower children**—baby boomers of the 1960s who were peace activists as symbolized by placing flowers in the barrels of National Guard rifles during campus protests.

- **hippies**—flower children who came of age in the 1960s.

- **swinging singles**—unattached and uncommitted singles who are characterized as thriving in a party atmosphere.

- **yippies**—self-styled radical activists of the late '60s and early '70s.

- **yuppies**—young urban professionals of the '80s with a taste for the good jobs and the good life.

- **new collar voters**—middle-class baby boomers who have neither the fancy titles nor fancy salaries of yuppies.

- **bright collar workers**—best-educated baby boomers who have snagged the best-paying jobs as managers and professionals.

- **dinks**—double-income-no-kids couples with great jobs and expensive lifestyles.
- **tweeners**—well-educated, young professionals caught between their low-rent roots and high-paying careers.

Not All Baby Boomers Are Yuppies

The label *yuppie* leaves a bad taste in my mouth. The fact is, no one likes to be labled, and we of all generations have had too many thrown at us. Although we have characteristics in common as a generation (the thesis of this book), no single label can define us. It is true that some people do fit the yuppie mold, but these individuals certainly do not represent the mainstream. One of the most serious mistakes anyone can make about our generation is to cast us all into that mold. Most of us simply do not drive around in Acuras and live a fast-paced lifestyle. In fact, only 5 to 8 percent of the population can accurately be called yuppies (Ingrassia 1986:13).

Richard C. Michael, coauthor of the recent Urban Institute Report to Congress on the economic future of the baby boom, explains:

> Most of those portrayed to be baby boomers tend to be urban yuppies, but they're not very typical. Baby boomers are more likely to be a young married couple earning $25,000 a year total, trying to raise one kid, postponing a second one and wondering how to buy a first house—or, if they are in a house, wondering how they can afford higher education for their kids. . . . The bulk of them aren't doing as well as their parents, though it's hard to convince people that something is amiss (Igrassia 1986:6).

The Tweener Backlash

Did you notice the word *tweeners* on my list of labels? It is an up-and-coming term for many baby boomers who don't want to be yuppies. Tweeners are among the growing number of baby boomers who resent being called yuppies. They work hard and don't want to be labeled as conspicuous, yuppie consumers because they try to live a sensible lifestyle.

Nikki Finke, staff writer for the *L.A. Times,* writes about these boomers in an article entitled "Tweeners" (January 24, 1988). She explains that the term *tweener* is not an acronym for anything but rather the invention of a New York journalist, working for ABC News, who borrowed the term from baseball. Just as a tweener in sports is a hit that falls between two outfielders, so a tweener—in a larger context—is a well-educated, somewhat successful and well-off young professional caught between his low-rent roots and his high-paying career.

Actually, tweeners have been around all the time but have not gotten all the attention that the so-called *yuppies* have received. One of the characteristics of this new classification of baby boomers is a strong tie to their roots. Whereas yuppies want to excel and go beyond many of their non-college-graduate parents, tweeners are proud of their roots, want to be like their parents, and enjoy old-style, traditional American values. They enjoy frequent trips back home to see Mom and Dad when they get vacation time—rather than flights to some exotic Caribbean island for a tan fest. One final note observed by Finke is that tweeners have a strong commitment to altruism. They like doing volunteer work and serving the needs of the community. This is good news for local churches, always in search for volunteers (Finke 1988:VI; 1, 10).

I see this latest trend, or perhaps we should say this latest identification of a massive subgroup within the baby boomers, as an encouraging one. Tweeners tend to be hard-working and committed to the family. They hold to many traditional biblical values and have strong loyalty and commitment to the heartland of America.

A Generation Still Searching for More

I find that baby boomers are still very much in search of their identity. A quick look at the media, full of explosive nostalgia that takes us back to the '50s and '60s, tells me that we're not sure where we're heading in the future. Sure, every generation gets hung up with nostalgia for a while, but when our children love the same music we loved in our teens, something is different!

Tom Shales, *Washington Post* TV critic, calls the 1980s the *"re-decade,"* a decade which lacks identity and so creates one by reviving, repeating, or just ripping off the past (Levine 1986:75).

Could it be that we've reached most of our goals by age 40, and we're not as happy as we were back then? We had a whole lot less then, but we stood for a whole lot more.

In an article, "Hanging on to the '60s," Beth Ann Krier, *L.A. Times* staff writer, talks about the outpouring of movies, TV, fashion, music, and protest that are "kicking into high gear an obsession with that delirious decade of the 1960s." Why is there an obsession with the 1960s today? Some suspect that the issues of the 1960s and the sense of purpose that our generation had in those days have never been resolved or fulfilled. The 1980s seem to depict a lack of purpose in our generation and an increasing feeling that materialism and prosperity are a dead end (Krier 1988:VI; 1).

Is the generation that has tried everything finally tired of trying? Now that many of us have reached the pot at the end of the rainbow, are we ready for more, for something deeper, for something beyond externals? Is this the cue for the church to redouble her efforts to learn, listen, and speak to the baby boomers? Is this a golden opportunity for the church to reap in the harvest of millions of boomers who might finally be ready to settle down with the truth?

Thinking It Through

1. Baby boomers have been the subject of much debate over the past few years. From what you have read in chapter 1, why are boomers worth discussing?

2. Baby boomers are different from other generations. What has shaped and molded this generation to make it unique?

3. At the end of chapter 1, questions concerning the lack of identity and purpose of the boomer generation are raised. What do you think about the author's basic conclusions? How do the Scriptures speak to this issue?

2

What's a Christian Baby Boomer To Do?

"You are the salt of the earth."
—Matthew 5:13

  I was interested to read the thoughts of Senator John Kerry of Massachusetts about baby boomers and their lack of purpose today. Here is a secular politician realizing that in many ways the wind is out of our sails at the moment. He believes that our social conscience went to sleep in the 1970s and if ever awakened, could change the face of America. It is still there, he believes, "but at the moment it is nascent. It has yet to be rekindled" (Thomas 1986:37). Shouldn't Christians be the first to wake up? Shouldn't Christian baby boomers be rousing the conscience of our generation? Unfortunately, the Christians of each generation usually follow the lead of the world. All too often the world succeeds in squeezing us into its mold.

  Today's secular baby boomers have adopted a pronounced and distinct value system. But what makes Christians of the same generation unique? I'm often hard-pressed to prove my lifestyle is any different than my unregenerate neighbor's lifestyle. But God calls us to be different:

25

Therefore, I urge you, brothers, in view of God's mercy, to offer your bodies as living sacrifices, holy and pleasing to God—which is your spiritual worship. Do not conform any longer to the pattern of the world, but be transformed by the renewing of your mind. Then you will be able to test and approve what God's will is—His good, pleasing and perfect will (Rom. 12:1-2).

We must be people who influence society rather than letting society influence us. Dr. J.I. Packer, recently addressing a commencement crowd at Wheaton College in Illinois, challenged the young graduating class to "put theology to work." He urged them to pursue a life of *nonconformist theological vitality*. I like that! In warning them against settling for personal material well-being as the supreme goal of life, he said:

We have to let our theology lead us in challenging, critiquing, and correcting the world's scale of values and the self-serving relativism that regularly goes with it . . . by an appeal to the unchanging absolutes of God's saving revelation (Halvorsen 1987).

Me and My Values

What are the values of our generation? We must identify them before we can challenge, critique, and correct them. And that is what this book is all about.

Values are clusters of attitudes, and baby boomers have bundles of these clusters. We have these attitudes about every area of our lives—relationships, the Christian life, politics, world events. . . . These attitudes added together form our *value system*. And our value system makes us act and react to life's circumstances in both positive and negative ways.

Where do we get our values? From our parents, peers, teachers, and of course the powerful media. The world around us shapes our values into what they are at any given time. And yes, they are fluid and dynamic, ever changing; however, most of us form our basic value system in our early years of life, say before we reach 25. That is why we baby boomers, especially the early crop, have values that still linger from the turbulent 1960s.

For a Christian, other major sources of value formation should come into play but are often weak signals when added to the already deafening roar of the other value-shapers. If I'm serious about my faith in Jesus Christ, my values should reflect my Christian beliefs.

But how do my values affect my action? On a daily basis, how do I act differently than my next-door neighbor Ernie (yes, a baby boomer too) who doesn't bother making Christ or church a part of his life? We both cut the lawn on Saturdays. We both watch our VCRs in the evening after the kids are in bed. We both shop at the same stores and visit the same beaches. He and I both struggle with the cluttered problems of raising a family on a limited income. What is different about me? What *should* be different?

Making a Difference Locally: Being Salt
What are we followers of Jesus (and baby boomers) supposed to do? One answer is found in Christ's Sermon on the Mount:

> You are the salt of the earth. But if the salt loses its saltiness, how can it be made salty again? It is no longer good for anything, except to be thrown out and trampled by men (Matt. 5:13).

Salt is *saline*, the most basic element of the life of the earth. It is found everywhere, including our bodies. It is even in my bottle of sterile solution for my contact lenses.

I use salt to clean my lenses, and God wants to use salt to spiritually and morally clean the world around us. When I was a child, my family spent many summer vacations at the beach in Florida. It was then that I first learned about the many values of salt. Mom would tell me that the salt water was good for any cuts I had on my feet.

Salt is a cleansing agent, but it is more. It is a preservative as well, and of course a spice to make food savory. And I believe that it is to all three of those roles that our Lord calls us. Jesus said that His followers *are* salt—really there is to be no choice in the matter. We are to be a cleansing agent, a preservative from evil, and spice to the world around us.

Not long ago I ran into an old friend who had been divorced for several years and was now involved with a woman he loved very much and wanted to marry. This new relationship was not going as well as he wanted it to, and he asked my advice. Both he and his girlfriend claimed to be believers, but I soon realized that they were not living that way. "Are you sleeping together?" I asked him.

"Yes . . . sure."

"Well," I responded in gentle but firm Christian love, "don't expect to come out a winner if you don't play by the rules."

His response impressed me: "Hans, we have both known that we shouldn't . . . but everyone does . . . and you're the first person that has had the courage to tell me point-blank what I know is really the truth."

Yes, we must be salt—gently yet firmly proclaiming God's truth.

A generation of 76 million baby boomers, rapidly becoming the leaders of our society, needs to be influenced. The contingency of believing boomers within that 76 million needs to be the primary agents of influence.

The majority of baby boomers have not been reached by any church. A poll by *People* magazine showed that baby boomers are half as likely to be in church on Sunday as the older generation.

Although many baby boomers are not attending church now, a recent Gallup poll says that 54 percent of the un-churched baby boomers in America are open to becoming involved in a church (Worcester 1987:1). Baby boomers are becoming more and more open to the Gospel. The oldest are hitting middle age and are questioning why they are unfulfilled in spite of all they have attained. Many are in their nesting stage of family life right now and are relatively open to the right kind of church, especially for their children.

As Christians inside America's largest generation, our task is clear. We must be salt.

Making a Difference Globally: Being Light

But Jesus not only called us salt. He also called us *light*. Again, He did not say, "Please be light"; He said we *are* the light—period. If we don't shine, there is darkness:

> You are the light of the world. A city on a hill cannot be hidden. Neither do people light a lamp and put it under a bowl. Instead they put it on its stand, and it gives light to everyone in the house. In the same way, let your light shine before men, that they may see your good deeds and praise your Father in heaven (Matt. 5:14-16).

The application here is quite simple and straightforward. We are a wealthy generation, 76 million strong, with the greatest resources any generation has ever had at its dispos-al. I look at our resources and conclude that we could move mountains for the cause of Christ if we'd get busy focusing on the needs of the world instead of our own needs.

The U.S. Center for World Mission in Pasadena, Califor-nia calculates that there are 17,000 people groups yet to hear of Christ. There is a crying need for evangelism, disci-pleship, and church-planting among at least half of the 5 billion people on the earth. Who better than our generation to help meet that need?

If the Me generation could again ignite its conscience to change the needy world, there is no limit to the impact we could make.

I received an interesting letter not long ago that captures the heart of what I am trying to say. A friend confided in me, "Lately I'm shocked to notice how much the thinking of the world (current baby-boomer philosophy) creeps into my own thinking. Learning to serve Christ instead of myself is indeed a battle." We have to come to grips with our values, evaluate them in light of Scripture, and then make the necessary adjustments in order to become salt and light for God's glory in the world where He has placed us.

We do that now as we examine baby-boomer values in a number of crucial areas.

Thinking It Through

1. Chapter 2 raised the issue of the contemporary values we encounter every day. After reading this chapter and taking a few minutes to let it roll over in your mind, make a list of 10 or 15 things you feel reflect the values of the boomer generation.

2. The sheer size of the baby-boomer bulge indicates the tremendous pressure and influence of this generation. What kind of value-related struggles do you face as you attempt to live out your Christian life around boomers?

3. This chapter suggests that there will be an ongoing conflict in your life as you attempt to establish and nurture Biblical values. Describe the role of rejection as you live out these biblical values.

4. In what ways have you, on a personal, individual level, had a biblically positive impact on someone in this generation?

3

Temptations of a Portfolio

"Money is power."
—Jerry Rubin

At the age of 33, Bill O'Donnell, Jr., had achieved the American dream—success in the corporate world. As vice president of Bally Manufacturing, he drew a $150,000 annual salary and owned an expensive house in Winnetka, Illinois with two Mercedes in the garage.

But he was cheating on his wife and using four grams of cocaine a day. He explained: "I was running through life so fast I didn't see that my role as a husband and father to my three sons was disintegrating, that my business abilities were crumbling" (Goleman 1986:8).

O'Donnell is just one of millions of aspiring executives—both male and female—lured into the fast lane by promises of power, prestige, and the big payoffs that come from a well-padded portfolio. (I am, of course, using the term *portfolio* here as the sum total of one's financial holdings.) Hollywood, television, and other advertising media try to convince the rest of us baby boomers that this is the great American dream for which to strive.

31

"Money Is Power"

In the early years of our generation, we were radically vocal about opposing the trappings of affluence and materialism, but 20 years later, we're busy beating Dad on the country club golf course. In the 1960s our motto was "I want to make a difference!" Today it seems to be, "I want to make a bundle."

There has been a not-so-subtle shift from idealism to materialism and hedonism. Jerry Rubin, one of the most celebrated leaders of the yippie movement of the late '60s, said of his generation then, "We ain't never gonna grow up. We're gonna be adolescents forever!" Today Rubin makes over $50,000 a year as a securities analyst on Wall Street and declares, "Money is power" (Thomas 1986:24).

Isn't it funny how the generation that seemed to care so little about money in the 1960s cares so much about it now? Back then ambition was out, taking life "easy" was in.

In the late 1970s Sarah Davidson, journalist and television producer, wrote *Loose Change,* a memoir of her journey through the 1960s. In a recent article in the *L.A. Times,* she wrote that the '60s were a time connected with "feeling young, feeling passionate, feeling good, and having time. Nobody has time these days to spend an entire weekend listening to music, lying on the floor, and hanging out with friends. In the 1960s, ambition was out. It was a dirty word. You had to hide it, but at the same time there was a sense that *you mattered;* that *values and morals mattered.* People felt that they could make *major changes in the world. That's been sadly missed in our lives"* (Emphasis added, Krier 1988:VI; 1).

Alexander W. Austin, a professor in the University of California at Los Angeles School of Education, has been tracking baby-boomer attitudes since 1966. Each year he sends out a survey to 300,000 college freshmen around the country.

Austin asks students to choose from a list of statements

that express what is most important to each of them. In 1967 just over 40 percent of the students surveyed chose the statement "being well-off financially", but by 1984 the number had climbed to about 70 percent. The number of students who chose "developing a meaningful philosophy of life" dropped from 80 percent in 1967 to 40 percent in 1984 (Makeower 1985:10-17). These statistics give credence to one person's notion that money is the long hair of the 1980s and that the altruistic values of the '60s are all but forgotten today.

The Pursuit of a Portfolio

Today the chase is on for ambitious financial accumulation. Much of the overzealous consumption among boomers today can be traced to greedy financial institutions. For example, just today I heard of a local car dealership that will sell me a shiny, sleek, new Ford (perish the thought that I should ride around in an old car!) for *no money down and no payments for one year!* Are these folks really just trying to be nice to me? No. If I went for such a deal, I would actually pay *twice* the original price of the car by the time it was all over. Ford gets their money, the dealership rakes in their share, and the bank gets rich off my interest payments.

In the last month alone, my wife and I have had three new credit cards thrown at us with no questions asked. We are good credit risks, so we can get these cards without even filling out applications. Why are we good credit risks? Because we pay our bills and stay out of debt. If these companies had their way, we would run up a horrendous debit on their cards and quickly become a poor credit risk!

Of course, people of all ages are bombarded by the ad media, but much of the attack is clearly aimed at the boomers who have the most money to spend today. We are the ones being pressured the most to borrow, spend, and accumulate.

Are All Baby Boomers Wealthy?

For about a decade, from the mid-seventies until the mid-eighties, young, urban, upwardly mobile, professional baby boomers (yuppies) were getting all the attention. They seemed to be the models for the whole generation; everyone that wasn't one wanted to be. But no more. It is a very encouraging sign to see many baby boomers reject the yuppie value system.

The fact is, as I mentioned in chapter 1, many boomers are struggling to stay afloat financially. Though it is hard to convince some people, baby boomers are not as well off as they might appear.

In his book *Boom! Talkin' about Our Generation,* Joel Makower states:

A very large portion of our generation can't afford to buy homes in the types of neighborhoods in which we were raised. And despite mind-boggling advances in the standards of living of most Americans in several decades of relative prosperity, many of us are worse off than our parents, at least financially (1985:10).

We early baby boomers have not been hit as hard as the late boomers born after 1957. Most of the older brothers and sisters in the boom generation got college degrees and good jobs and bought houses before the economy soured in the 1970s and before the prices of houses soared out of sight. There were just too many of us competing for the same jobs, added to a major recession in the early '70s, the oil crisis, and almost a decade of double-digit inflation until the Reagan years.

Financial times for the baby boomers are not as good as they look to outsiders. Many moderate-income boomers are looking to the 1990s with scaled-down financial expectations. Many of us recall with a certain sense of wonderment our parents' ability to buy a home, enjoy a comfortable standard of living, and raise three children all on *one income*.

Learning to Change Our Models

We may disdain the yuppie label, but we will still be tempted by the glitz and glamour of the good life that is constantly paraded before our eyes by the secular media. The pressure is on to buy things we don't need with money we don't have to impress people we don't even know! We must learn to tune out what we see on TV, in magazines, and at the movies. We must focus on other models.

In a *Christianity Today* article, Chuck Colson offers a sobering word of caution:

> We Christians are not immune to the seduction of money, success, power and prominence. Far more often than we would care to remember, the church has girded itself for battle against the world—only to discover that the enemy is within. Evidence abounds today that this pattern is repeating itself, as the church dallies with the false values of an egocentric and materialistic culture. So as we preach to the yuppie let us beware: cross-pollination will only produce our own crop of yuppies—young, urban, pew-sitting professionals whose faith is but a notation on their resumes and whose ornate churches are but a reflection of their social status (1985:20).

Our model for dealing with wealth and a personal portfolio should obviously come from the Scriptures. God must have known that every generation would struggle with wealth because the Bible is full of good advice on money.

We can also learn much from the model of godly people we know who are living out a biblical set of values. When we spend time with people who are making a difference for Christ—or read good books about them—we gather the courage to do the same.

A portfolio is a place where we gather together all our investments, our net worth; it is a place where we can see the external value of our earthly riches. I have a hunch that God keeps a portfolio on each of us as well, and of course, the contents are quite different. There He stores up a record of the treasures we've laid up in heaven, the good works we have done for His good and His kingdom.

Don't Dream about Winning the Lottery

On the radio yesterday a news broadcaster spoke with envy and excitement about someone here in California who just struck it rich: "Today, California has another millionaire, as So-and-so of Stockton picked all six numbers in the weekly lotto." That kind of news causes millions of Americans to spend their grocery money on the gamble of the state lotteries. We all want to be wealthy.

Being wealthy is not a sin. But the Bible does say that allowing wealth to replace God in our hearts is a sin.

In his 1987 commencement address, Dr. J.I. Packer warned Wheaton College students:

> Gazing into my crystal ball, I foresee that when you step outside Wheaton, the pressure will be on you to identify with what we nowadays call "yuppiedom." You will find it the easiest thing in the world to settle for personal material well-being as the supreme goal of life (Halvorsen 1987).

Maybe many of us boomers are not as well-off as people think we are, or as well-off as we would like to be. But the pressure is on to become that way. The trend is for boomers to become more and more affluent as they approach the peak earning years in the coming two decades.

As Christian baby boomers, we must be on guard against materialism. We must follow a few important biblical principles regarding wealth.

1. *Guard against the apathy of affluence.* There are many admonitions in the Scriptures about the curse of wealth. It seems that throughout history, the church has always become the most anemic in times of greatest material prosperity. When Constantine made Christianity the official state religion of the Roman empire in the fourth century, it was the beginning of the end. The wealth and success of the church destroyed it. Conversely, the fires of persecution have purified the church. Jesus warns the affluent believers in the church of Laodicea:

> You say, "I am rich; I have acquired wealth and do not need a thing." But you do not realize that you are wretched, pitiful, poor, blind, and naked (Rev. 3:17).

Why does this happen? Because we seem to think that when all is well on the *outside,* all is fine on the *inside.* When we have no material needs, we quit our praying—we cease to depend on God and seek His face. We must be careful not to be lulled to sleep by a false sense of security, the apathy that so often accompanies affluence.

2. *Value your relationships above money.* No amount of money can replace peace and love in a home. But how much energy in the modern boomer home is put on gaining wealth while the family structure crumbles? How often is Dad out there killing himself trying to get things for his children when all they really want is *him.* A Gallup poll revealed that 50 percent of divorces are related to financial problems and overextended budgets (Thomas 1987:19). Proverbs 17:1 reminds us: "Better a dry crust with peace and quiet than a house full of feasting with strife."

3. *Rub shoulders with those less fortunate; the more you've got, the more you need to give.* Arrogance is an easy trap of the wealthy. But believers who have money are not to hide in their country clubs and affluent neighborhoods but to go out and help the poor. Most of us *are* wealthy

37

when compared to people in the rest of the world.

The more we have, the more God holds us responsible to give. And in God's way of looking at things, the more we give away our riches, the more we will experience true life! Paul writes:

> Command them to do good, to be rich in good deeds, and to be generous and willing to share. In this way they will lay up treasure for themselves as a firm foundation for the coming age, so that they may take hold of the life that is truly life (1 Tim. 6:18-19).

I'm not a proponent of rich Christians giving all their money away and becoming poor. That is not a biblical concept. But I do believe that believers have a great responsibility to give generously of their wealth and their talents. The answer is a graduated tithe: the more you get, the more you give. John Wesley put it this way: "If those who gain all they can, and save all they can, will likewise give all they can, then the more they gain, the more they will grow in grace, and the more treasures they will lay up in heaven" (Niebuhr 1929:28). This principle is illustrated in the life of a friend of mine named Johann, who struck it rich in Silicon Valley in Northern California. He made millions and had all that money could buy, then he lost it all. It was while at the bottom of his failure that he found Christ and had his life put back together.

At that point, Johann made a promise that few keep: "Lord, if you help me get back on my feet I'll give you all the glory." But he has kept his promise. In a new job he quickly took an ailing computer corporation into the black in the span of a few short months. When his first of several bonus checks of $10,000 each was given to him by the board of directors, he told them, "This money belongs to Jesus Christ, for it is He who has really made me successful here." Imagine saying something like that in front of all those pin-stripers in a stuffy corporation boardroom! The Sunday that I spoke in his church in San Jose, he handed the pastor that $10,000 check as a testimony for all to see. I think his message was much more powerful than mine that day.

4. *Dream about winning the ultimate prize.* We need to focus not on winning the lottery but on winning God's approval. We should approach life, including our financial affairs, so that we will be welcomed to heaven with the words, "Well done, thou good and faithful servant."

The New Testament story of the widow and her offering (Luke 21:1-4) speaks to this truth. The story is so close to my heart because of the numerous widows who have sacrificed for the success of our ministry overseas. Just last month I performed the funeral service for such a dear saint whose name was Dorothy. This precious elderly woman gave of her limited income for seven long years to help fund our ministry in Europe. I know that her reward in heaven will be great. Baby boomers, let's learn some lessons of sacrifice from these dear old saints.

5. *Focus on the secret of godly contentment.* Finally, the clear call of Scripture is to focus on the value of obtaining godliness: "But godliness with contentment is great gain. For we brought nothing into the world, and we can take nothing out of it. But if we have food and clothing, we will be content with that" (1 Tim. 6:6-8).

We do not need more money; we need to be more like God. Who is blessed in God's eyes—the wealthy person? No. In God's eyes the poor in spirit, those who mourn, the meek, those who hunger and thirst for righteousness, the merciful, the pure in heart, the peacemakers, and the persecuted are the blessed ones. This is God's economy. As Christian baby boomers, the passion of our lives should be *God's peace,* not the world's vain pursuit of a fattened portfolio.

Thinking It Through

1. Describe what you feel to be the success model of the boomer generation.

2. How is a biblical model of success different from that which is presented to us via the media?

3. What are you doing to shape your success model more along the lines of Judeo-Christian values?

4

Caught in a Fitness-crazed Generation

"Eat Like a Pig. Look Like a Fox."
Recent ad for Low-Cal Yogurt

In 1962, *Life* magazine reported that astronaut John Glenn ran two miles a day to keep in shape. People were amazed! It seemed incredible that someone who wasn't a professional athlete would run that far and do it every day. Now, over 25 years later, more than 20 million runners, mostly baby boomers in their thirties and early forties, run four or five miles several times a week. It used to be that if you saw a man running down the street in his shorts at 6:30 A.M., you wondered if he was either insane or running from his wife! But no more. Now, early morning commuters have to be careful not to run down the jogging masses on the roadsides.

In high school, sports were the very last of my interests. I was in the long-haired crowd, a member of a rock group, and one of the many of my generation who played around with drugs during those turbulent years of the '60s. The sports "jocks" were seen as our arch rivals. In all my years of schooling, I was never on any athletic team. When I went off to college at the University of Alabama, I spent my time at sit-ins and campus demonstrations, not at football games and fraternity houses. That was the 1960s, but my how things have changed in the 1980s.

In 1986, I ran my first marathon—me, ex-doper and long-haired radical. I ran 26 miles without stopping! Who would ever have imagined? I have a good friend in Dallas who was a star football player in high school and college. When we have a chance to jog together, I take great delight in the fact that I can beat him: ex-quarterback defeated by ex-hippie! I am in much better shape today in my late thirties than I was in my twenties; in fact, I'm in better shape than I've ever been.

So what happened? Why am I running and eating granola instead of bacon and eggs for breakfast? Why such a change not only in my life but also in millions of my generation?

Reasons behind the Fitness Rage

In a current TV commercial, aimed squarely at baby boomers, a young woman talks about turning 40. "Do you think I'm going to take turning 40 gracefully?" she asks the viewer. "Not on your life. I'm going to fight it all the way!"

How? With Oil of Olay, of course!

Many baby boomers seem to have decided that fitness is even more effective than Oil of Olay in staying young. Why this obsession with fitness? Why has *this* generation become obsessed with staying young?

Some good answers come from trend analyst John Naisbitt, author of the bestseller *Megatrends*. As we entered the 1970s, Naisbitt explains, Americans lost faith in the ability of medical science to cure all our physical ailments. The long promised cure for cancer didn't arrive. People began to shift their faith to the areas of fitness, diet and nutrition, believing that a stronger body could resist disease better (1984:146).

Another major force behind the fitness rage is the change in the way so many of us now work. America used to be an industrial and agricultural society without any joggers. After working all day at a physical job, who wanted more exercise off the job? Most jobs today do not require strenuous, physical activity. In fact, more and more of us are working at sedentary information jobs. We are pushing paper instead of a plow. So to stay healthy, we must exercise.

It is clear that as society has changed, we have changed our habits about our own physical well-being. According to Naisbitt, at least 100 million Americans, almost half the population, are exercising in some way, up from a quarter of the population in 1960. One in seven Americans now jogs on a regular basis (1984:147).

Even corporate America supports the fitness craze. Many companies, small businesses, and factories have constructed gyms, fitness parks, and recreation areas for their employees. They are realizing that this fitness and health rage, largely fueled by baby boomers, is more than a passing fad. It is here to stay.

A Changing Outlook on Health

In many ways the baby boomers are leading the trends in fitness and health. Since 1965, for example, we have reduced our fat intake mightily: we consume 28 percent less butter and 21 percent less milk and cream (Naisbitt 1984:147). Today, Americans consume 15 pounds more chicken, a pound more fish, and 22 gallons more low fat milk per capita than they did in 1976. Beef consumption has fallen off sharply. Dr. Robert Haas, author of the well-known books *Eat to Win* and *Eat to Succeed*, says this lean cuisine trend will continue. He predicts that in 20 years we will still be eating all the same foods, but they will contain substitutes for most of the fats (Rosellini 1986:60). Just recently we have received reports that the NutraSweet Corporation, maker of the popular sugar substitute Equal, has come out with a revolutionary new fat substitute product. We will soon be able to eat fat without getting fat!

Americans are even smoking less. The American Cancer Society concluded that the number of smokers in the United States has dropped by 50 percent in the last 25 years. Today, just 25 percent of men and women over 40 are smokers.

Part of the change in our outlook on health and fitness is increased medical knowledge. Even though Naisbitt might be right when he claims that we have lost faith in the ability of the medical establishment to cure all our problems, we do benefit daily from the dramatic progress in medicine. We are the first generation not to die of such childhood diseases as polio and the measles. We are the first generation for whom childbirth poses little risk. We have grown up hearing almost daily about radical medical advances, such as artificial hearts and liver transplants. The result of all this knowledge has been an increased lifespan. The average life expectancy of male baby boomers born in the 1950s is about 66 years, compared with 53 years for our fathers born in the 1920s. That is a gain of 12 years in one generation! Males born today have a life expectancy of over 72 years. For women, the change is even greater. Women born in the 1920s had a life expectancy of 60 years, but boomers born in the 1950s can expect to live 73 years. Little girls born today, like my Cambria Michelle born in 1987, can expect to live to over 80 years (Johnson 1988:796).

Beyond life expectancy, we boomers have also changed what I call "prime expectancy." Because we are staying in better physical condition than previous generations, we will push back the years of retirement and sedentary living, greatly increasing our years of vigor and productivity, known as the prime of life. We are staying younger longer.

In Search of the Fountain of Youth
Our attention to fitness and health so clearly reveals our obsessive search for the fountain of youth. We are deter-

mined to be forever young. The media fuels our quest by creating advertisements which are hourly compelling us to buy the clothes, cars, medicines, foods, and fitness programs that will keep us looking and feeling like a 20-year-old.

"If you don't like your body, change it!" is the latest craze. Plastic surgeons are making a dramatic comeback as we enter the decade of the '90s. Baby boomers now willingly submit themselves to a surgeon's table in the hope of looking younger.

I recently came across an advertisement from a plastic surgeons' medical group. The doctors offered to perform the following types of reconstructive surgery:

> Breast Enlargement
> Fat Suctioning
> Nasal Surgery
> Eyelid Surgery
> Facelift
> Tummy Tuck
> Cheek/Chin Implants
> Breast Lift
> Breast Reduction
> Ear Surgery
> Hair Transplants
> Dermabrasion
> Reconstructive Surgery

This is not just the stuff of Hollywood and movie stars; this is a rapidly growing industry across our land, being indulged in by an increasing number of people! Why, those sags, wrinkles, and bulges can be removed in moments by a quick visit to your local body-fixer. Major unflattering folds and flab can now be restructured or even removed with the controversial method of liposuction—a fancy name for fat suction. Take a little out there and squirt it back in over here where I need more form.

Putting Fitness in Perspective

The other day my son Mark came home from kindergarten with a funny story to report to me. That morning I had made him his standard peanut butter and jelly sandwich. Apparently, when he ate the sandwich at lunch in front of his best friend Chad, he ran into some major opposition. As we walked home from school together, he explained the conflict: "Daddy," Mark began with a sigh, "Chad's daddy says that peanut butter and jelly is bad for you because it's full of sugar and salt. Is that true?"

Oh, brother, I thought to myself, *this is getting ridiculous.* I calmed Mark's fears. "Don't you worry about it, Mark!" Some things are sacred in my book, and no one is going to take away my Jif and Welche's.

There is no doubt in my mind that for many baby boomers this health fitness fad has gotten out of hand. Millions of boomers are flooding fitness centers, worshiping their bodies by trying to obtain and maintain a 20-year-old physique. Fitness is fine. Eating healthy foods is good. But what about the *inside* of a person? The bottom line is that we are giving less and less attention to quality on the inside—character, ethics, inner beauty, and spirituality—and placing more and more emphasis on externals. We are healthier than any previous generation, but there is a shallowness that has come over our generation, perhaps because we have had it too easy and been handed too much.

The greatest danger in all of this fitness focus is to judge people by external appearances. That *is* the way the world judges but should not be the practice in our value system. In the kingdom of Christ, it is the inside that counts:

But the Lord said to Samuel, "Do not consider his appearance or his height, for I have rejected him. The Lord does not look at the things man looks at. Man looks at the outward appearance, but the Lord looks at the heart" (1 Sam. 16:7).

As Christians inside America's largest generation, we must develop a biblical response to this fitness craze.

1. *We must examine our motivation for being fit.* We serve God through our bodies, and we are admonished to glorify Him in our bodies. If we are in poor condition and take lousy care of our bodies, we are often severely restricted in how much we can do for the cause of Christ.

I believe that God is pleased when he sees Christians taking better care of their bodies. But when we begin to worship our bodies by putting them above more important priorities, then we have fallen into the trap of the Greeks, who idolized the human physique.

Body worship is a source of major pride among baby boomers today—another extreme in our culture to guard against. I must ask myself what my underlying motives are. Why am I working on my body's condition and appearance? To impress others? To look more attractive to someone? To look younger? Am I motivated by externals or internals: am I trying to impress others with how I look, or am I maintaining a healthy stewardship of the only body God will give me this side of eternity?

I find that a certain degree of physical conditioning is great for my personal discipline in all other areas of my life. A balanced emphasis on keeping in shape and eating food that will enhance our health is certainly God-honoring.

Do you not know that your body is a temple of the Holy Spirit, who is in you, whom you have received from God? You are not your own; you were bought at a price. Therefore honor God with your body (1 Cor. 6:19-20).

2. *We must maintain a balanced perspective.* Consider the following statements:

God made us physically the way we are. We need to thank Him for our bodies. If we are overweight couch potatoes because of our own laziness and gluttony, then He is pleased if we do something about it. But if we try to make our body more or less than He made it, then we are unbalanced:

> You created my inmost being; you knit me together in my mother's womb. I praise you because I am fearfully and wonderfully made; Your works are wonderful, I know that full well (Ps. 139:13-14).

The inside—under the skin in our hearts, souls, and personalities—is more important than what we see on the outside. Isn't it funny how much time we insist on spending in front of the mirror each morning, getting ready for the day. Appearance is the golden coin of self-worth in our society, reinforced through hundreds of messages we receive each day. But in God's way of looking at things, it's the inside that counts.

> Train yourself to be godly. For physical training is of some value, but godliness has value for all things, holding promise for both the present life and the life to come (1 Tim. 4:7-8).

Physical fitness does not equal spiritual fitness; spiritual conditioning should come first. Being a jogger, I love getting the "runner's high," that euphoria which elevates my senses to a higher plane as I run long distances. I also enjoy watching performances of great athletes, like the star of the 1988 Olympics, Florence Griffith-Joyner, better known as Flo-Jo. To watch her run was almost a spiritual experience, seeing the ultimate in performance of a body God designed in His creative genius. But physical conditioning really does not connect me to God or improve my relationship with God unless I let the discipline spill over into spiritual exercise. Men and women through the ages have tried to gain spirituality by physical discipline and denial, but to no avail:

> Such regulations indeed have an appearance of wisdom with their . . . harsh treatment of the body, but they lack any value in restraining sensual indulgence (Col. 2:23).

Face it, our bodies are going to get old. One of my favorite professors in seminary was Dr. Howard Hendricks, who often stressed, "Men, if it is the *physical* that holds your marriage together, then every year your relationship is going to get worse!" It is ultimately futile to try to look and stay young as we age, for God has programmed our biological clocks to run down:

> You sweep men away in the sleep of death; they are like the new grass of the morning—though in the morning it springs up new, by evening it is dry and withered (Ps. 90:5-6).

Impress people with your inner beauty. One of the main reasons I was attracted to my lovely wife was that she had a beautiful interior to match her attractive exterior. We boomers are the most designer-conscious of any generation, but these outward labels mean nothing in the character arena:

> Your beauty should not come from outward adornment. . . . Instead, it should be that of your inner self, the unfading beauty of a gentle and quiet spirit, which is of great worth in God's sight (1 Peter 3:3-4).

3. *We must learn to respect the golden years.* We are probably the first generation that has tried to take the age out of eldership. Throughout the Old and New Testaments, however, much is said about the wisdom that can come only

from advancing years. The leaders of both the Jewish community and the early church were known as *elders* for a good reason—it was assumed that age brought wisdom. There are many things in life that simply can't be mastered at a young age or seen through the eyes of youth.

In the eyes of eternity, old age is nothing but a step closer to our perfect fellowship with Jesus Christ and the acquisition of our new bodies. I'm looking forward to hanging up my jogging shoes! But in the meantime, I'm asking God to help me grow old gracefully and accept the physical aging process as part of His plan and pattern for my life.

As the old man Moses prayed in his advanced years, "Teach us to number our days aright, that we may gain a heart of wisdom" (Ps. 90:12). As I read that, I conclude that the more *days* I live, the more *wisdom* I acquire, so growing old is nothing to fear and nothing to hide. Turning 40 won't really be terrible. In fact, deep down, I'm looking forward to getting older because I need more of the wisdom that aging brings.

Thinking It Through

1. What has happened during the boomer generation which has nurtured the growing emphasis on personal physical fitness?

2. Describe the contrast between the biblical values presented, related to fitness and our bodies, and what you face as presented by peers and media.

3. What do you do to maintain a healthy balance between honoring God with your body, wanting to change your body, and growing older?

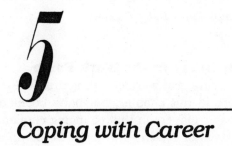

Coping with Career

*"The Organization Man is dead...
but ambition is alive and well."*

Whether we work at home or in an office, most of our waking hours are spent in labor. I suppose we have Adam and Eve to blame. Because of their disobedience, they were cast out of the Garden of Eden—a true workers' paradise—and pushed into the world where all of us now survive by "the sweat of the brow."

Today, in the final years of the twentieth century, we are seeing perhaps the greatest changes in the nature of work since that revolution from tending the Garden to toiling in the fields.

For a long time our view of work in America was: the husband goes off to work and the wife stays at home with the family. The reality of the matter today might be: man and his wife go off to work, dropping the children at a day-care center on the way. Or consider these variations: man dials up his office over the modem and works until evening, or man gets home to feed the kids, and his wife goes off to work.

51

The Boomer Bulge in the Work Force

Not only is the nature of work changing drastically today, as we will explore in this chapter, but baby boomers are becoming the major players in that changing climate. According to the authors of *Re-Inventing the Corporation*, "Baby boomers are now populating the ranks of top management. By 1990, they will comprise 54% of the labor force in America" (Naisbitt and Aburdene 1985:7). As our generation grows to greater dominance, our values will be strongly expressed and felt throughout the organizations in which we work.

Theory Y and the Boomers

Before we look at boomer values in the workplace, we must look at two underlying currents that have shaped the values of this generation. One began back in the 1960s, the other in the 1980s. The first was a movement popularized by a man of the older generation, Douglas McGregor; the other by the futurist, Alvin Toffler.

Until his death in 1964, Douglas McGregor was the Sloan Professor of Management at MIT—a very prestigious post. His book *The Human Side of Enterprise,* considered a classic in business schools, popularized his *Theory Y* approach to management. Today, 30 years later, his book is still a bestseller and has an enormous impact on management thought in America.

In McGregor's book, he contrasts two ways of looking at leadership: *Theory X,* the old idea of control and dominance over the worker; and *Theory Y,* a more cooperative partnership with the worker.

Based on a new look at human nature and also on motivational theory, *Theory Y* encompasses the beliefs that work can be *enjoyable* and that management should respect and trust workers enough to let them direct and control their own tasks. *Theory Y* is best understood when contrasted to *Theory X* because it was developed as a reaction to the tight structure, control, and accountability of the old traditional *Theory X*. The following chart sums up both viewpoints (Hersey and Blanchard 1982:49).

THEORY X	THEORY Y
1. Work is inherently distasteful to most people.	1. Work is as natural as play, if conditions are favorable.
2. Most people are not ambitious, have little desire for responsibility, and prefer to be directed.	2. Self-control is often indispensable in achieving organizational goals.
3. Most people have little capacity for creativity in solving organizational problems.	3. The capacity for creativity in solving organizational problems is widely distributed in the population.
4. Motivation occurs only at the physiological and safety levels.	4. Motivation occurs at the social, esteem, and self-actualization levels, as well as physiological and security levels.
5. Most people must be closely controlled and often coerced to achieve organizational goals.	5. People can be self-directed and creative at work if properly motivated.

Although most baby boomers may not know it, they have been influenced by *Theory Y*. The focus on the nature of human relationships and the integration of personal goals with the success of enterprise makes sense to the value system of this generation. Boomers want their work to have meaning and emphasize relationships instead of authority. Most boomers are not willing to work at a job that they dislike year in and year out, just to live for the weekends and holidays and retirement. Instead, they speak up and speak out.

Third Wave

In the 1980s, Alvin Toffler popularized the second current that is shaping the values of baby boomers, the idea of *The Third Wave*, in his book by that name. Like *Theory Y*, this concept has also shaped boomer values in the workplace.

Toffler suggests that our society has shifted from an industrial focus to an information/technology emphasis. The first wave of our society was the agricultural era, the second was the industrial revolution, and today the third wave is our focus on technology and information. This latest shift in society has forced a dramatic change in management styles, part of which Toffler calls the *Third Wave*. Again, to simplify the concepts, a chart is worth a dozen pages. The following chart (Sculley 1987:95) was developed by James E. Cook, president of Computervision Corporation, and compares the management characteristics of second and third wave companies.

Contrasting Management Paradigms

Characteristic	Second Wave	Third Wave
ORGANIZATION	Hierarchy	Network
OUTPUT	Market Share	Market Creation
FOCUS	Institution	Individual

STYLE	Structured	Flexible
SOURCE OF STRENGTH	Stability	Change
CULTURE	Tradition	Genetic Code
MISSION	Goals/Plans	Identity/Direction/ Values
LEADERSHIP	Dogmatic	Inspirational
QUALITY	Affordable Best	No Compromise
EXPECTATIONS	Security	Personal Growth
STATUS	Title and rank	Making a Difference
RESOURCE	Cash	Information
ADVANTAGE	Better Sameness	Meaningful Differences
MOTIVATION	To complete	To build

As we will see in the following section, many boomers have bought into the Third-Wave way of looking at things.

Changing the Way America Works

There's no doubt about it. We are working differently than our parents did. Some of the change is because of the times in which we live, and some is because of who we are as a generation. An article in *Businessweek* explained:

The emerging conflicts (between the older generation and

the newer) are not just a matter of numbers. The baby boomers have different attitudes toward work. Those values are reshaping corporate cultures—what many see as a "greening" of management. The shift to participatory decision making, teamwork, flexibility, and autonomy is often attributed to adopting the apparently successful Japanese style of management. But it may be a direct outgrowth of dealing with the 60s generation of workers (1984:53).

Whatever the reason, many baby boomers are changing the way America works.

CAREER CHANGES. We are a very energetic and vigorous generation, largely due to our physical fitness. As a result, we will have a different middle age than our parents had. Because of our expanded adult prime, one career expert says, "People will have two, three, or four sequential careers, instead of just one. They'll work at something for 20 years, then feel it's time to get out, go back to school, and start again. It's happening now, but the baby-boom generation will be doing it even more" (Ingrassia 1986:8).

As baby boomers age, we will reshape many views about retirement. We will work longer and be a greater influence in the workplace than any previous generation.

THE DEATH OF THE ORGANIZATION MAN. In his famous book *The Organization Man*, (1956), William H. Whyte wrote that a corporation is the place to stay the rest of our lives. But boomers see the corporation largely as a place where they want to achieve certain personal satisfaction within a certain amount of time. They are committed to professions but often not to a particular company.

In a *Newsday* article, Michelle Ingrassia explains:

Unlike their fathers, they [baby boomers] have resisted

being molded by the all-seeing, all-knowing corporations; instead, they are molding corporate America in their own image. Better educated, they're more inquisitive and more eager to have a say in their jobs. Competitive, they are writing their own definitions of success. Impatient, they are unwilling to spend 40 years climbing through the corporate ranks. They are the generation trained to want it all—and they want it all now (1986:8).

THE DEATH OF THE INFALLIBLE COMPANY. Baby boomers have not only developed a new way of looking at their roles at work but also a new view of companies themselves. *Individuals,* not *institutions,* are the focus of Third-Wave thinkers. And *networks,* not *hierarchies,* are the glue that holds organizations together.

My dad worked for NASA most of his later career, and he got upset with people inside the organization from time to time. But he generally held the organization in high esteem and felt that it was not the organization's fault itself when things went wrong. Many companies are realizing today that baby boomers have a completely different view of the organization. If these younger workers are not respected and appreciated for their contribution *(Theory Y),* then they leave. Robert Foster, Grummund Corporation's deputy director of personnel and administration, explains this greater demand for meaning and dwindling respect for corporations that he sees in the boomer work force:

It used to be that when a foreman or supervisor said to do something, a person did it and didn't ask why. And they looked at the company as being somebody, some entity, that would pretty much be right in the way it approached things, especially if it was a good company. In the last 20 years, people are not as willing to be directed to do things. They will do what you tell them to do, but they want to know why and they ask, "Is there another way we can do it better?" and "Do I really have the visibility of knowing what is going on in my company to satisfy myself that I should be doing what I'm doing?" It's a feeling that the corporation is not necessarily the all-seeing, all-knowing entity that it used to be, that it gives you an opportunity to use your talents, but you have to look out for yourself, too (Ingrassia 1986:10).

THE MYTH OF THE SOLE BREADWINNER. Without a doubt, the greatest change that baby boomers have brought to the workplace is the employment of women outside the home. Today 53 percent of the work force is female. And in 66 percent of young married couples from age 25 to 34, both husband and wife work. In 1973 the figure was only 47 percent (Thomas 1986:26).

Most married baby boomers have kept up with the standard of life their parents enjoyed only by depending on two incomes. According to a report released by the Joint Economic Committee of Congress in May of 1986, if it were not for the 50 percent increase in working women that joined the work force between 1973 and 1984, the drop in average family income during that period would have been three times greater than it actually was (Ingrassia 1986:9). These working women make middle-class suburbia possible for baby-boomer families.

Of course this change for women has not come without cost. It has created a whole new problem in the clash of children and career. *Time* magazine calls these working women "Super Moms," and speaks of a psychic guilt tax that is deducted from their paycheck (Thomas 1986:35). In chapter 8, we will take a closer look at the issue of working mothers. It is not an issue we can ignore.

The Truth about Our Work
Now, as Christians inside America's largest generation, how do we respond to all these changes and pressures? I draw

several conclusions from my present understanding of baby boomers and their world of work:

1. *If you are in a position of leadership, respect your followers.* If there is one good trend that our generation has brought into the workplace, it is respect for the dignity of the individual. Life is full of work, but that doesn't mean that it has to be miserable and demeaning. McGregor's *Theory Y* has helped elevate all of us who work for a living to a place of dignity, regardless of where we are in an organization. McGregor's management style emphasizes giving employees *utmost respect* and treating them with the *dignity* they deserve, not as some mere machines of productivity. Sound familiar? Here is what Jesus had to say about it:

> You know that the rulers of the Gentiles lord it over them, and their high officials exercise authority over them. Not so with you. Instead, whoever wants to be first must be your slave—just as the Son of Man did not come to be served, but to serve, and to give His life as a ransom for many (Matt. 20:25-28).

One clear way we can be salt in our workplace is to follow Christ's example and treat those who work for us with respect and dignity.

2. *If you are in a position of followership, respect your leaders.* I must admit, on behalf of my generation, that at times we have allowed the pendulum to swing too far away from respect for authority. Events like Vietnam and Watergate have undermined our respect for authority. Maybe our problem with authority comes from being let down and wanting now to take our destiny into our own hands. Whatever the reason, most authority figures are experiencing great difficulty gaining a following, and that is a problem in our generation.

The Scriptures are clear that God uses authority to mold

us and discipline us, and that we are to respect those whom God has placed above us in authority. Some of the best and yet most painful lessons I've learned in my adult life have come through learning to respect and submit to authority over me. I have streaks of rebellion all through me, left over from the '60s, that still want to get in the way of my growth to maturity in Christ.

Not long ago I was discussing with a good friend an authority problem that I had at my work. I told him that I had contemplated resigning and going elsewhere where I would be wanted and respected for who I am. With cutting love, my friend said, "Hans, if God wants to make you a diamond, then He is going to chisel away your rough spots, using His authority over you. If you throw away this hammer [present authorities over me], don't you think He'll pick up another one in the next place you go?" Powerful words that we boomers don't like to hear! God teaches clearly from Scripture that He expects us to respect and submit to both sacred (1 Thes. 5:12) and secular leaders (Rom. 13:1) as those whom He has placed over us for our own good.

3. *Have you considered settling for less?* The older we boomers get, the more the pressure of ambition is on us. If I let off in the drive to keep up with my peers, the gap between us widens to a great gulf. Could it be that God might demand that we live on the down side of such a gulf in order to pursue His priorities for our lives? It is a radical, painful choice that I believe He wants many of us to make.

It is interesting to see the kind of men that Jesus chose as His apostles. He did not seem concerned about what they *did* for a living, but He did care about what they were *like* on the inside. His board of directors was not stacked with bankers, lawyers, and wealthy businessmen. He Himself was content—that is a key word in this discussion—to be a carpenter and continue His trade. As He once told His followers, "My food is to do the will of Him who sent Me and to finish His work" (John 4:34).

In God's eyes, wealth doesn't matter: "What good is it for a man to gain the whole world, and yet lose or forfeit his very self?" (Luke 9:25)

I have been encouraged to see a number of my peers turn down promotions or transfers because they didn't want to hurt their family life. I believe that God smiles on such decisions and blesses such commitments. At times, we must count the cost to our spiritual and family life—it might be better to quit or settle for a lesser position to maintain our priorities.

Just a short time ago I lost one of my best friends to his career. It was devastating for all of us. His career became such an obsession that he lost everything else on his climb to success—his wife, two little children, and his faith. And by the way, he didn't reach success either. He went from being a godly husband, caring father, and responsible church lay leader to a life of misery in adultery. It all began by working more and more hours to climb the career ladder in his company. He would leave for work before anyone was awake and get back to the house when the kids were already in bed, too exhausted to pay any attention to his wife. His supervisor made him work Saturdays; it was expected of him if he was to get ahead.

During the middle of this crisis, after he had moved out of his home and in with his girlfriend, he sought my help. He wanted to come back and get things right. I went directly to what I saw as the cause of the cancer that drove a wedge between him and everything that really mattered. "Bill," I said (I've changed his name), "the best thing you could do to save your life and your marriage is quit your job. I would rather see you sweeping streets and living in an apartment—back with your family and back in the church—than in the job you now have with all its perks." That was too much for him to consider, and he is now divorced from his family and gone from all our lives.

Thinking It Through

1. How has the workplace changed from when your parents started their first jobs?

2. Describe the differences between the X and Y theories of management as discussed in this chapter. How might biblical values be blended together with these theories as you perform your duties in your career, whether it be in or out of the home?

3. While people around you derive their sense of worth from pouring their lives into their jobs, how do you balance work, family, friends, and God in your own search for a sense of worth?

6

Owning without Being Owned

"He who dies with the most toys wins."
Bumper sticker

Recently I was shopping at a mall in Southern California and noticed a new store going in next to Target. Although the interior of the boutique was far from being ready for business, the brightly colored red sign was already in place: **The Cozy Yuppie.** I suppose yet another merchandiser is climbing on the bandwagon by catering to the purse of the baby boomer. After all, we boomers are the ones with the strongest buying power. Ask any businessman.

In chapter 3, "Temptations of a Portfolio," we talked about money, but now we turn to the baby boomer's obsession for the *things* that money can buy. The pursuit of wealth in itself is an important issue, but of equal and parallel importance is the issue of preoccupation with things, things, and more things.

The Power of Media Hype

By 1990, *every other household* in America will be headed by a person born between 1946 and 1964. These baby boomers will be responsible for *50 percent of all consumer spending*. That means we will all be hearing a lot more about our generation in the growing onslaught of media hype, aimed at the boom generation. Have you noticed how many television commercials use 1960s music to sell products to the children of the '60s?

When we realize that two thirds of all U.S. economic activity revolves around consumer spending, then we can see just how important baby-boomer spending is. It drives the entire U.S. economy. Business and industry need us— desperately. They are hiring the best in the advertising business to sell us everything from small computers to big BMWs.

The problem with the media hype is that it creates unrealistic demands in us, the consumers. Of course, the favorite image in many advertisements is the yuppie—young, well-off, mobile, living in the fast lane, and at the center of success. Although, as we have already established, yuppies are only a small group of baby boomers with which most people our age don't really want to identify, the media continues to tempt us with that materialistic image of success. The reality is, most of us could not afford to keep up with the yuppies if we wanted to.

One *Herman* comic strip explains the situation so well. Herman is lying on a psychiatric couch in deep despair. His psychiatrist says, "I'm having a difficult time understanding the source of your anxiety. You have a luxury townhouse, a motorhome, three cars, a powerboat, all the latest stereo and video equipment, and you're planning another vacation in Hawaii."

"I only make $85 a week," Herman sighs (Unger: Nov. 1, 1987).

Me-ism and Materialism

Whether or not we can afford it, many baby boomers have unfortunately bought into the pursuit of materialism. It is all part of being the Me generation.

A 1986 *Time* magazine article, based on a survey of baby boomers, examines our materialistic generation:

> From the first, the baby boomers were accustomed to instant gratification. Often brought up in shiny new suburban enclaves of middle-class comfort, they were doted on by parents who were counseled by Dr. Spock to dispense with the rigidities of traditional child rearing. Their surrogate parent was the television set. Parked in front of the glowing blue tube for an average of four hours a day, a quarter of their waking life, boomers became the first video generation.
>
> Bored? Just change the channel. Hopping from one instant fad to another—from Davy Crockett coon skin caps to Hula-Hoops—they moved as a single mass, conditioned to think alike and do alike. Trendiness became a generational hallmark; pot to yoga to jogging, they embraced the In thing of the moment and then quickly chucked it for another (Thomas 1986:24).

We are affluent, many of us, but we can't afford all the things people want us to buy, and we don't *need* these things anyway. Even more important, we must learn that materialism is destructive to life in the Spirit.

Shut Off the Messages

CBS News reported in 1988 that the average American receives 5,000 messages a day from the combined sources of all media. Although we remember only 1 to 3 percent of that information, the overload tends to keep us ever considering what purchases we'll make next. And who do you suppose most of this media onslaught is aimed at? The baby boomer, of course, who holds a clearly targetable 50 percent of the spending power of all consumers.

A few weeks ago I conducted a junk mail survey in our

home, just to get a picture of how many messages get inside my house even if I don't turn on the TV or radio.

Within two weeks the big box by the front door was overflowing. The results of my survey were disgusting. I finally decided I wouldn't even count them all: dozens of sweepstakes offers; hundreds of pages of advertisements from local stores; dozens of restaurant coupons; dozens of retail store shopping magazines; all kinds of direct mail ads for everything I could ever dream of wanting but don't need; and then a whole raft of little flyers hung on the doorknob every day by real estate agents, lawn services, print shops, and reroofing salesmen. The point is, I could spend all my time just going through all this mess deciding what I need and don't need. And *that* is the problem. Why bother? The advertising media try to occupy many of our waking hours with just having to make choices.

We have to learn to shut off the messages. Or how else can we ever have time for the important, unseen priorities?

Turning to Scripture, we read about young David, a man after God's own heart, who is a role model for Christians tempted by materialism. David didn't have junk mail and TV to contend with, but certainly he faced equal temptations in his day and in his position. But when he was a young man, he demonstrated how to live life in pursuit of the right priorities. He explained:

Blessed are they whose ways are blameless, who walk according to the law of the Lord. Blessed are they who keep His statutes and *seek Him with all their heart*.

I seek You with all my heart; do not let me stray from Your commands.

I rejoice in following Your statues *as one rejoices in great riches*
(Ps. 119:1-2, 10, 14, emphasis added).

What Are We Devoted To?

I will never forget the day I drove off to college as a young freshman. I was leaving home, 18 years old, and on my way to the university. In my tiny VW bug was my sister, who was also a student, and everything I owned . . . *everything*. And for about five years (until I got married!) I could always get everything I owned in the VW. For me that was freedom, and I was happy without a house full of things that seem to tie me down. Now, 20 years later, I spend many of my waking hours fixing, cleaning, straightening up, working to pay for or replace objects mistakenly labeled *conveniences*. There is great wisdom in the old saying, "That which you own will eventually own you!"

In the affluent, materialistic society in which most of us find ourselves, the temptation to allow possessions to possess us is at every turn. We daydream about that new car or stereo we're going to buy, or how we will decorate the home as we get more money. But God is a jealous God, and His first commandment is: "You shall have no other gods before Me" (Ex. 20:3). Another Old Testament reference reminds us: "Be careful, or you will be enticed to turn away and worship other gods and bow down to them" (Deut. 11:16).

But wait, you might say, I'm not bowing down to worship my possessions; I haven't made my things an idol.

The word *idol* is defined as "any object of devotion." Now we are hitting too close to home. *Devotion* is attention—focused attention. To worship an idol is to give too much attention to that "thing," to the exclusion, neglect, or avoidance of that which should have our first allegiance.

Now, I can have many things and not idolize them, but the potential and temptation is ever before me. Every time I go to the mall, I see new things jumping out of store windows, begging for my affections. The television, radio, and print media are constantly offering up new dishes of appealing products, clamoring for my affections and my devotion.

I remember when I bought my first computer. I know it became an idol. It received most of my devotion/attention for weeks before it arrived as I pored over the brochures that described it. Then once it arrived, it took most of my energy and all of my time for months. At night I would lay in bed thinking about new things I could do with it. In the morning I would wake up so eager to sit back down at the keyboard that I would skip my devotions (notice how we use that word in this context) because I was too impatient and too focused on that machine. My computer became an idol.

Of the many images that Jesus used to portray spiritual points, one of my favorites is the image of water in His conversation with the Samaritan woman. He uses the image to speak directly to this issue of what we devote ourselves to.

Everyone who drinks this water will be thirsty again, but whoever drinks the water I give him will never thirst. Indeed, the water I give him will become in him a spring of water welling up to eternal life (John 4:13-14).

Material goods never satisfy. We always want more.

The Mesmerizing Power of Materialism

How much of our time do we devote to servicing, fixing, cleaning, arranging, and paying for all those things that are supposed to make life easier and simpler?

The fact is, these things make life more complicated and cluttered. And, worst of all, they dull us into a false stupor of security and complacency. Materialism by its very nature is external, and by our obsession with it, we neglect the internal dimensions of life. This builds on top of the fitness craze, another emphasis on the outside, and pushes us further from devoting time to the inside issues of the heart.

This conflict between the external and the internal was a

problem for the church in Laodicea, one of the churches addressed in the Book of Revelation, and the church believed by many Bible experts to be the model of the church in the last days before Christ's return. Our Lord warned:

You say, "I am rich; I have acquired wealth and do not need a thing." But you do not realize that you are *wretched, pitiful, poor, blind, and naked* (Rev. 3:17).

Imagine that, people rich in every good material thing being accused of being poor, blind, and naked! If there is a serious danger that wealth has brought to the church in the affluent West, it is the mesmerizing complacency of thinking that everything is fine on the *inside* because we have it so good on the *outside*.

Fighting Materialism

For Christian baby boomers, the pressure to keep up with fellow boomers is one of our most intense battles. We should remember that earthly possessions mean little in God's kingdom. Consider the following suggestions:

1. *It's OK if you don't drive a BMW.* When we came home to the States after our six years in Vienna, one of our supporters graciously offered to buy us a car. Now who are we, homebound missionaries, to look such a gift car under the hood? Well, the car was a 1978 Malibu—over a decade old. Now I happen to love cars—nice cars. It has been a great exercise in eating humble pie to sit at the red lights and glance over to see my baby-boomer neighbor beside me in his shiny, black BMW 325i. At a moment like that, the nonverbal communication is deafening! His glance in my direction says it all: "What a loser ... driving that old bomb."

What did Jesus say? "Life does *not* consist in the abundance of things [or their relative age and cost]." So try this test on for size. If you have a friend (or grandparent) who has an old bomb of a car, trade your shiny new car with them for a week. Or if you can't part with yours, park it for a week and just borrow a bomb. See how different you feel when you've changed the externals? See how much our possessions are a statement of our worth? See how much pressure there is on us to have the latest status symbols? Let's be different. Why should the world squeeze us into its mold? Of course, we all don't have to drive bombs. But if a life packed with luxury fills us with pride (a natural response), then we would be wise to do with less.

In the fitness chapter we saw that the greatest danger of the fitness focus is judging people by external appearances. This is even *more* true when it comes to the things people own. That *is* the way the world judges, considering us of *more* value if we own more and better things. But in the kingdom of Christ, it is the inside that counts:

> But the Lord said to Samuel, "Do not consider his appearance or his height, for I have rejected him. The Lord does not look at the things man looks at. Man looks at the outward appearance, but the Lord looks at the heart" (1 Sam. 16:7).

2. *Learn to shut off the media hype.* It is possible to severely cut down those 5,000 messages we receive each day. We don't have to watch TV every night; we don't have to keep the radio on to fill up the quiet in our lives. We don't have to cruise the malls with our spare time, inviting the consuming monster to bite us.

I solve the junk mail problem easily. I always read my mail over the wastebasket. Unless I know I am looking for a good deal on a specific purchase, I don't even look at the advertisements. I toss them. I have decided that *I* will determine what *I* need. To spend an hour every day going through all the ads, coupons, and great deals only wastes my time and tempts me to buy things I don't even know I need! Why even expose yourself to the battle when you don't have to? The best policy for battling the advertising onslaught is "out of sight, out of mind."

3. *Try living within your income, not your credit line.* If there is one thing baby boomers are guilty of, it is spending beyond our means. And why not? Everyone is pushing new cars—with no money down—and credit cards down our throats. The lenders of our society want us to live above our means because they get rich off the interest we pay them. The Scriptures are clear on what that produces: "The rich rule over the poor, and the borrower is servant to the lender" (Prov. 22:7).

Today the personal debt level in the United States is increasing at the rate of *$1,000 per second.* The Federal Reserve Board estimates that consumers spend one out of every four dollars in American income to keep up with installment debt. Living this way puts tremendous pressure on marriages.

4. *It's OK to de-accumulate.* I believe that the less we cling to our things, the more we'll be blessed by God. And at times that may mean giving up some things, doing without the latest and the best and the most—and even giving away things to others who have need.

A good friend of mine told me of an amazing story of a group of Christians who did just that. He goes to a church in Birmingham, Alabama that raised the *entire* funds to build a new sanctuary in two weeks' time. I admire them first of all for not wanting to go into debt, which has destroyed many a church. But the method they used to raise the money was most unusual; it reminded me of some Old Testament stories. When there just wasn't enough money coming in, people began to bring things instead of money. Valuables like jewelry, cars, antiques, and even deeds to stocks and property were brought as offerings to pay for their new building. It was the greatest spiritual renewal that affluent congregation ever experienced. Why? Because for those weeks, they let go and gave with reckless abandon.

5. *Adopt a better status symbol.* If there was ever a generation hung up on status, it is our generation. We live with designer everything, from briefcases to kids' clothes. Many of us are so possessed with being "in" and "with it," that we spend large portions of our waking hours just processing the information that will help us stay with it and keep up with our boomer neighbors.

I propose a different value for Christian baby boomers, or at least a value of higher priority. It is the value of the *internal and eternal riches.* Today God is looking for baby boomers who are in search of inner excellence. That is His ultimate value as He measures our spiritual status, and in the long run, that is all that will count. But, oh, how we hate the long run—we who are in love with instant gratification.

Consider these words of wisdom from Jeremiah which put the status symbols of our modern society in proper perspective.

This is what the Lord says:
"Let not the *wise* man boast of his wisdom [knowledge/ education/expertise] or the *strong* man boast of his strength [athletic ability] or the *rich* man boast of his riches [financial and material success] but let him who boasts boast about this: that he understands and knows Me, that I am the Lord, who exercises kindness, justice, and righteousness on earth, for in these I delight," declares the Lord (Jer. 9:23-24, paraphrase added).

Thinking It Through
1. How is the accumulation of things related to idols?

2. Why is the accumulation of things such an easy trap into which we fall?

3. What steps can be taken to develop and nurture a better status symbol for yourself?

7

The Computer Revolution

"The computer is a bicycle for the mind."
—Steven Jobs, founder of Apple Computer

In 1981 my wife and I moved to Europe as missionaries. Shortly after our arrival in Austria, I touched a computer keyboard for the first time: a Radio Shack TRS Model III. Within weeks, my new boss in Vienna told me, "Hans, you need to buy yourself one of these."

"Me, buy a computer!? Whatever for?" I asked in amazement.

That was in the early '80s. Today, few people question the value of using a computer. Times have changed dramatically in less than a decade, and now homes across our land have not one but two picture tubes glowing in their homes at night: the TV and the PC.

It is getting harder and harder to resist contact with the buttons and video screens of computers. They show up everywhere. The change in just the last five years has been staggering.

Here is an example of what a day might look like for me: In the morning, on the way to the office, I stop by the bank money machine and punch a few buttons for some cash. Of course, most of my work at the office is on a word processor, and I am linked to our other offices by fax and electronic mail. At noon, I go to the library to look for some books, checking the optical laser disk on the new computer card file for my titles. Later, I stop by the mall and punch in the kind of merchant I'm looking for in the mall directory. In the record store, I punch up an audio/video search for the album I might want to buy. Even if I don't know the exact name of the album or the artist, a close guess will find the selection on this "smart" system. Stopping by the gas station, I punch in cash and amount on the pump and pay with my ATM card. Donna called me and asked me to stop by on the way home and pick up a few groceries. Yes, you guessed it! The grocery store has electronic checking at the checkout; they just swipe my card through and punch in my secret code, and the groceries are paid for. In the evening, I can call the bank and talk to its computer by pushing buttons on my phone to see if I still have money for all those transactions! Then I record the bills I've paid on the spreadsheet in my PC.

It is impossible to avoid the computer revolution.

The Technological Wave of the Future

Personal computers are taking the place in our generation that cars used to have. People used to talk about their automobiles. But today men and women are just as likely to be talking about megabytes, floppy drives, optical laser disks, laser printers, and the comparative values of various color monitors.

In 1982, I bought my first computer, and for my money I got a black and white screen, two floppy disk drives, and 64 thousand bytes of internal memory. And I was very excited about that computing power. But in 1988, for less money, I purchased a new generation of computer with 256 colors in the screen, processing speeds thousands of times faster, two floppy drives, 2 million bytes of internal memory, and a hard disk drive with 43 million bytes of memory! We are clearly in the middle of a technology revolution. The drastically cheaper and more powerful computers are fueling the information revolution as it gets easier for more and more people to process vast amounts of information.

Baby boomers are leading the charge into the technology revolution. In fact, in many ways we're causing it, starting up company after company that feeds the fuel of the technology transition. Steven Jobs, famous baby boomer, who was worth millions before his 25th birthday, began it all when he and his friends invented the first mass-marketable PC, the Apple computer. John Sculley, CEO of Apple Computer, in his book *Odyssey,* chronicles that exciting adventure: "The personal computer industry was an industry created by and for a new generation" (Sculley 1987:141).

Personal computers are not just the sophisticated expensive toys of a spoiled generation, they are what the future is all about. They are helping to usher in what Alvin Toffler calls the *Third Wave* of revolutionary social change in Western countries. In his book *The Third Wave* (1980), Toffler describes three great waves of change in human societies, the third of which is upon us now. They are what he calls periods of great ruptures of social forms in civilization.

The first great wave of change on our planet occurred at the end of the *agricultural era* of society, a stable period in the history of man that lasted for thousands of years until the end of the seventeenth century. At that time Western societies experienced the upheaval which swept across most of our planet as the *industrial revolution* began. That period, according to Toffler, lasted about 300 years—until our present generation. It is now coming to an end. In the mid-twentieth century, the third great transition period began, bringing upheaval in areas of technology, economics, politics, family life, energy use, and many other areas of social life (Toffler 1980:13-14). Though harder to label than the agricultural and industrial revolutions in Western society, I would label this transition that is upon us as a *global technology/information revolution*.

The place we feel these changes most is in our jobs. Work is an integral part of life in every corner of our globe. And as we saw in the chapter on careers, the way we all work is changing dramatically. Very few of us will ever have the kind of jobs our parents did.

In the agricultural era, we had what would be called *no-collar workers*. Everyone worked the earth by the sweat of their brows to make a living. No one wanted or needed aerobics classes or jogging shoes. Then the industrial revolution brought the masses into urban areas and ushered in the *blue-collar workers*, the great industrial centers, and labor unions. Finally, in our generation, we are seeing the demise of industry and the explosion of high technology and information, producing a nation of *white-collar workers*.

It is interesting to notice the way people have resisted change between these eras just described. It is human nature to resist change. The farmers fought the industrialists during the expansion of industry, especially in the late nineteenth century. And now, many of the older, traditional, heavy industries are fighting the onrush of the information revolution. Blue collar jobs are unfortunately becoming unnecessary, so many workers must be retrained or lose their jobs.

The same tension that existed between the old farmers and the new industrialists also exists today between the old industrialists and the new technologists. Members of the older generation aren't so sure they want their world changed that much. But most baby boomers, as a generation, have accepted this third wave of the future enthusiastically.

Transition to Technology
Technology is making dramatic strides in our generation—

enough to leave all of our heads spinning as we try to keep up. There is a growing fear among many that if they don't keep up, they will be left behind in the technology revolution. Old jobs done manually for decades are disappearing weekly, and those who are not boning up on how to make the transition to technology and the PC may just be out of a job forever. John Sculley writes of this transformed way of working:

> As we move into the information economy, the desktop, not the factory floor, is becoming the workplace of the future. Increasingly, workers are at desks utilizing their minds, instead of at factory machines using their hands (Sculley 1987:377).

A good case in point is my friend Jim, whom I have known for about 10 years. When I first knew him, he was an expert at working with sheet metal fabrication. Every day when he came home from work, he was dirty from working out in the shop and often had cuts and bruises from the metal work. I talked to him the other day and was amazed at how things have changed in his shop. He doesn't get dirty anymore. He does all the design work on a computer. And most of the fabrication is done by computerized machines as well. A clean factory floor of button pushers.

Marvin Cetron, President of Forecasting International Limited, gives us these interesting and revealing facts about the nature of work and communication in the not too distant future:

> By the year 2000, 88% of the population will be involved in service industries. Half—44%, will be in the information fields. Half of those people will be working at home or be able to work at home because of interactive cable. What accounts for these changes? Between 1969 and 1984, for example, 90% of all medical advances took

place—meaning that a doctor, researcher, or surgeon who hasn't read the literature only knows 10% of what is going on. If you take a look at materials for instrumentation, cars, houses, automobiles—90% of every single thing we have in materials research came out in the past ten years. So the information component becomes extremely important, and, therefore you've got to be able to communicate, write, read, analyze, and solve problems (Johnson 1988:86).

Personal Productivity and the PC

Yes, the computer has in many ways added to our uneasiness about the changing world in which we live because it is one of the prime culprits of change. But the computer is here to stay, and many of us have no choice but to get computerized. Most of us are drowning in information. The total amount of information in our world is multiplying and quadrupling at a staggering rate. Can *any* of us keep up with the paper and print messages thrown at us daily?

Because so much information is flooding into our lives, it is imperative that we learn how to use computers to weed through the information in order to use that which is necessary. If we ignore the technological revolution, we will at best be left in isolation and ignorance; at worst we might lose our jobs to those who know how to handle information.

I don't know how many times I have said to my colleagues, "I'm glad that I am living in the age of personal computers—otherwise I could not get a third of the work done that I do." Christians are often the last ones to take advantage of new tools for their mission. We can use the computer, like the printing press or the airplane, to more effectively reach our world for Jesus Christ. For the church and those boomers being asked to lead it, ignoring the technology revolution will create an enormous gap between Christians and the world they are trying to reach. The problem will be twofold: they will be less able to relate to their world, and they will be less efficient in reaching it with their message.

The Bible and the PC

During the late 1970s and into the 1980s many Christians resisted computers on spiritual grounds. I recall reading articles that warned churches not to computerize, using the rationale that the Holy Spirit should not be limited by such worldly inventions. I'm sure there are still a few fringe groups who would condemn its use. But I can't recall the last time I've been in a church office and not seen a computer busy at work keeping records and disseminating information crucial to the church.

Many pastors today are creating their message outlines on computers, giving them the ability to polish and repolish their thoughts at lightning speed. After the sermon, they can go back to their study, call up the outline from the disk, and instantly zap the illustration that just didn't work right. Next time, the message will be better, thanks to the new ease that a communicator has to polish his thoughts before and after presenting them.

As with all of man's inventions, the computer can be used for good and evil.

The Limits of PC Power

George Orwell was wrong. Nineteen eighty-four came and went, and Big Brother did not take over our society with the power of the computer, even though the computer has advanced far beyond the dreams of Orwell. But we are certainly living in an age of computers, and I can safely say that there is a computer in your future.

As Christians living in an age of computers, we must be careful. Those who have vast amounts of knowledge through their use of computers can certainly control individuals in a tyrannical way. The computer can indeed bring into society great dangers to personal freedom. It can also foster pride in people who become skilled in manipulating this tool.

But the computer, used appropriately, can help both the church and individual Christians gain knowledge that will yield greater productivity for the cause of Christ and His church. As helpful as computers may be, we do need to keep our use of them in perspective with the kingdom of God. We must be careful not to make an idol of this helpful tool. Consider the following statements:

1. *Computers may or may not increase our effectiveness.* Efficiency is defined as *doing things right,* whereas effectiveness is *doing the right things.* I know I have wasted many days trying to be efficient through the use of my computer, while I neglected more important tasks that God wanted me to do to be effective for Him. We might want to post the prayer of Moses above the monitor of our PCs:

> Teach us to number our days aright, that we may
> gain a heart of wisdom (Ps. 90:12).

2. *Computers are not a cure-all and should never replace the human and divine aspects of problem solving.* Some people would like to think that computers will solve any problem. Their motto is: if the organization has any needs, throw a computer at them. But technology and information do not solve all of man's problems.

We should remember that the *power of prayer* and the *working of the Holy Spirit* in a life, a family, and an organization must take precedent over any human tools invented to solve problems. Could it be that at times we are robbing ourselves of a blessing because we are not waiting on God to work for us? Instead, we are busy engineering our own feeble solutions. Can you imagine Joshua and his followers trying to build a bridge across the Jordan instead of waiting and watching as God dried up the flooded river for His people? (Josh. 3)

David, the mighty warrior, learned the secret of true power in problem solving. In his day, the horse and chariot were symbols of superior strength for warfare; whoever had the most ruled the land:

Now I know that the Lord saves His anointed;
He answers him from His holy heaven
with the saving *power of His right hand*.
Some trust in chariots and some in horses,
but we trust in the name of the Lord our God
(Ps. 20:6-7).

3. *Computers can become a nuisance in our ministry and family*. I have seen the computer become such an obsession in some lives and organizations that it destroys relationships and good working conditions. In an organization, the computer can get more attention than the needs of the people, which is wrong. Perhaps a worker will not get a new desk, but the computer will get a $2,000 disk drive.

Much to my despair, I learned right after I bought my secondhand computer from a man in California that the computer was the source of his separation from his wife. He had become so obsessed with that machine that he spent his family's limited income on more and more additions to the computer system. Finances destroyed the marriage.

I know that Donna has the hardest time getting through to me when I am deeply engrossed in a computer project. It is as though I am engaged in combat with the machine, unable to give up until I solve the problem. At times I must simply turn off the computer and tend to the needs of the people around me.

4. *Computers can become a dangerous source of pride*. We know that knowledge is power, and he who controls knowledge is very powerful in any organization. It is humorous to watch the power that a secretary can have over the boss because she knows how to get the information he

needs out of the computer, and he doesn't.

The danger comes when the power of knowledge is used in a prideful way. This is exactly the danger Paul was warning the Corinthians of when he said, "Knowledge puffs up, but love builds up" (1 Cor. 8:1).

Later in Corinthians, Paul sets all of this in perspective:

If I have the gift of prophecy and can fathom all mysteries and all knowledge, and if I have faith that can move mountains, but have not love, I am nothing (1 Cor. 13:2).

Thinking It Through

1. Why does the author so strongly make the point that computers are not just expensive toys but the building blocks of the future?

2. Describe five advantages and five disadvantages of becoming computer-literate.

3. How has becoming familiar with a PC at work or home helped or hindered your relationship with God, family, friendships, work, and recreation? How can a computer best assist you as you seek to grow in the Lord and keep up with our ever-changing world?

8

Marriage under Fire

"A marriage will never last that begins with this vow: 'I will stay with you for as long as I shall love you.'"
—James Dobson

Ed and Marguerite are two very special friends of mine. Happily retired and in the golden years of life, they are busy serving in their church. They are fun people to be around. But what I really enjoy about Ed and Marguerite is the beauty of their marriage. They just celebrated their 45th anniversary last week, yet they act like young lovebirds. I take my hat off to people like these two because I know how difficult it is to have a good, lifelong marriage.

I have purposely waited until this chapter to take up the issue of marriage because the tremendous pressures on baby-boomer family life can best be understood against the backdrop of what we have discussed in the previous chapters.

Many baby boomers have failed miserably in the area of marriage. But interestingly enough, as we will see in the next chapter, many baby boomers shine when it comes to raising their children. Our generation seems to be more committed to making children turn out right than making marriages work.

What Happened to the Nuclear Family?

In the early 1980s, futurist Alvin Toffler wrote about the death of the nuclear family—a typical family of four in which the father functions as the breadwinner and the mother as a homemaker. Many baby boomers grew up in this kind of family.

According to Toffler, the nuclear family now exists in only 7 percent of U.S. homes. If we broaden our definition of the family to include those in which both spouses work, and those with one child or no more than two children, we are talking about only 25 percent of American households (1980:211).

Recently I was waiting in line at a department store and overheard two women in front of me discussing the upcoming marriage of one of them. I noticed nothing unusual about their discussion until I realized that the woman about to be married had been living with her boyfriend for a couple of years and was just now planning a formal wedding. Although this situation shocked my ears, it is not an uncommon practice. A taboo in the '50s is now a widely accepted practice in the non-Christian world.

An article entitled "Baby Boomers Come of Age" reports that the social stigma of living out of wedlock has become a thing of the past:

> The census bureau reports that the number of unwed couples has risen from 523,000 in 1970 to 2,220,000 in 1986. Most of these couples are young (65% under 34) and have never been married (52%), but many have been divorced (34%). They tend to be more educated than the general population and put education and career before marriage and family. Some will later marry, but in the meantime, they all enjoy the emotional security the

arrangement provides, without the legal or economical restrictions of marriage (Johnson 1988:791).

Having lived in Europe for a number of years, I often see trends in the U.S. that follow the pace set by the more humanistic and secular societies of Western Europe, which have had a few more decades in what Francis Schaeffer called the "post-Christian era." For example, in Sweden, cohabitation is four times as popular as in the United States (Johnson 1988:791).

One of the tragic breakdowns of the nuclear family is the growing number of single-parent households. In 1986, one in every six households was maintained by a woman with no husband present. (This figure applies to women who are: separated, divorced, widowed, or never married but raising children.) By contrast, in 1960 only one in ten households was maintained by a single mother.

Another variation away from the traditional nuclear family in our society today is a new class of baby boomers who have chosen to be childless, giving them the newly coined label, Dinks (double-income-no-kids). These couples don't want to clutter their lives with the pressures of parenthood. They want freedom to pursue their careers, unencumbered by anyone or anything, much like many singles that we'll discuss in chapter 10.

In our modern society of the late twentieth century, we are by no means seeing the total elimination or "death" of the nuclear family. But from now on the nuclear family will be only one of the many socially accepted means of establishing a household.

That is cause for the church to stand up and take notice. The traditional ministry approach of speaking only to the needs of the nuclear family will meet less and less of the needs of the population. The church must learn to reach out in new ways to the millions of people living in these new arrangements.

The Marriage Mess

The breakdown of the nuclear family clearly stems from the breakdown of marriage. The institution of marriage is a mess today, especially among the baby boomers.

In my research I have found that we are definitely doing worse than any previous U.S. generation in the area of sticking with a marriage partner. In the 1960s, the failure rate of marriages in America was 25 percent. One out of every four marriages ended in divorce. But in the 1980s, the U.S. Census Department reports that the rate has shot up to 48 percent: today one of every two marriages ends in divorce (Johnson 1988:786). According to the National Center for Health Statistics, the divorce rate in America went through the roof when we came of age.

The bottom line is that *baby boomers are the ones getting all these divorces.* The median age at which people divorce is 34 for men and 30 for women. Many of us have friends or family members who have gone through the hurtful process of divorce. It is a sad trait of the times that litters the landscape of our generation.

As boomers came of age in the 1980s, a whole set of factors began to put pressure on their marriages. Boomer marriages began to fail at an unprecedented rate. In some ways we could say that every change our generation has faced, described throughout the pages of this book, has put destructive pressure on baby-boomer marriages. We now turn to one of the biggest culprits.

Why Two Incomes?

No change within our generation has had more of an effect on marriages than the rise of the two-income family. Perhaps many people in the older generations don't really understand why so many mothers work today. The unfair simplistic answer is to say that baby boomers are selfish and want too much. It is much more complicated than that.

Why is it that so many baby-boomer husbands and wives

both work? Is it really a matter of greed or a matter of necessity?

It is actually an economic necessity if boomers want to live anywhere close to the standard of living their parents enjoyed. Consider these facts: according to the Population Reference Bureau, medium family income, which totaled about $14,000 in 1947, rose by more than $5,000 during the 1950s and by more than $6,000 in the 1960s, reaching a peak of $28,433 in 1973, measured in constant dollars. But by 1984, the medium family income actually dropped to $26,167 (Igrassia 1986:9).

Many older people outside of the boomer generation have misunderstood the problems facing young, two-income boomer couples today. They think someone failed and that we are all too greedy, when actually, the entire economy has shifted so much that one person can't earn enough to meet the needs of a family. Of all living costs, no expense has risen more than housing costs, driving many single-income, young couples right out of the market. Things are particularly hard for younger baby boomers.

Working Women

Before we had children, my wife, Donna, had a very successful career, first as an executive secretary and then as an administrative assistant to a manager in the oil industry. She loved her seven years of work and received a great deal of praise and affirmation from her career. Now she works inside the home. The work is harder and the hours are longer.

Donna has chosen to be a homemaker but would sometimes enjoy the pace of the office environment. She could rest if she went back into the oil business! Work at home for a woman who is a wife and also the mother of four children is some of the hardest work around. Unlike most jobs outside the home, "results" in the lives of young children are not usually obvious, nor are they immediate. If it were going to be easy to raise kids, it never would have started with something called "labor."

In recent years both of us have felt the subtle psychological pressure, even from Christians, for Donna to work outside the home. I can recall on a number of occasions that other women (working mothers mostly) have treated Donna as somewhat backward, ignorant, and less than complete because she chooses to stay at home.

Consider these statistics:

• *The number of married women in the work force has doubled over the last 30 years.* In 1950, census figures showed that 31.4 percent of all women and 24.8 percent of all married women were in the work force. By 1984 the number had soared to 54.4 percent of all women and 54.7 percent of all married women (Ingrassia 1986:2).

• *More and more mothers are working outside the home.* In 1950, 28.3 percent of all women with children worked outside the home. By 1960, the number had climbed to 39 percent, then in 1985 the number of mothers working outside the home jumped to 67.8 percent (Ingrassia 1986:2).

• *Child care crisis.* In a segment on "The Child Care Crisis," ABC News reported that 60 percent of the women who work outside the home have children under the age of six. That means that every working day 10 million children are put into day-care centers in America. Most of these kids have baby-boomer parents (May 11, 1988).

Granted, many mothers are working because of economic necessity, but others are working to build a career and to find worth. An article in *Chatelaine* magazine entitled "Baby Boom Women: High Hopes, Uncertain Prospects" speaks about women's new attitudes toward work, marriage, children, and self-fulfillment. Gray explains that the income of working women gives them the power to influence consumer trends. In fact, women now have more impact on their generation than women have ever had. But Gray goes on to explain:

Now, in their late 20s or early 30s, many are experiencing an emotional barrenness in serial relationships and career commitment, and a gnawing sense of dissatisfaction with their lives (Gray 1983:68).

Carol Orsborn, a 39-year-old public relations executive explained the dilemma this way: "I don't care what I have to give up. I want to make my life authentic." She and her husband had the "model" baby-boomer marriage: co-ownership of a successful public relations firm, a dream house on San Francisco Bay, and two children. Although they seemed to have it all, she admitted, "I just didn't feel I had anything."

Fed up with the frantic pace and lack of fulfillment, Orsborn cut her work week from 70 hours to 30, much to the horror of her husband. She began to take time for herself and her children. She finally admitted, "I just couldn't believe I was trapped by my own liberation." Orsborn went on to found Superwomen's Anonymous and write a book: *Enough Is Enough: Exploding the Myth of Having It All* (Anderson 1987:VII:18).

There is no estimating the social, psychological, economic, or spiritual impact of women—especially mothers—who go into the work force. It has far-reaching impact on our whole society, and it affects the family unit directly, the basic building block of our society.

Saving the Endangered Species of Marriage and Family

The major changes in society make the family feel like a punching bag with each new external force taking a blow at the already weakened and fragile family core. As society in general values the family less and less, Christians must fight to maintain a strong home. Probably the biggest challenge facing Christian baby boomers with growing families is to maintain a healthy marriage and strong commitment to wholesome family life. Many forces are working against our best intentions.

In a day when we have more light on the subject than ever before, why are marriages failing at a worse rate than ever before?

Sometimes I think we're victims of double jeopardy. On the one hand, we are bombarded by the secular media picture of an outwardly appealing and romantic marriage which is, in reality, impractical, unrealistic, and unobtainable. Then on the other side of the coin, we are bombarded with books, sermons, and radio shows that tell us the standards for a "Christian" marriage. Add all the books and sermons together, and they equal frustration. The standards are so high that a great deal of frustration sets in when unrealistically high hopes are not met. It is simply communication overkill.

On the one side marriage is painted by the media as too romantic, but on the other it is built up as too spiritual. Finding a survivable middle road is increasingly difficult for young Christian families.

Am I going to offer my perfect solution? Hardly. The last thing I want to do is add to the guilt trip of struggling Christians, trying to make a go of a marriage dedicated to survival, enjoyment, and the glory of God. I offer here a few guidelines that my wife and I have found to be effective in building a marriage that works and gives glory to God. It is not a perfect list, for there are no perfect marriages.

1. *View marriage from a biblical point of view.* There are two ways of viewing marriage that seem to me to be at opposite ends of the spectrum. One is the view from the media and Hollywood, where couples fall romantically in love and walk blissfully off into an emotional sunset hand in hand. Deep down we know this is just make-believe. The other viewpoint is from the reality of the Bible, where we find principles for a love that really does last a lifetime.

Hollywood romances are ficticious and fickle; the Creator gives us the real story on love and marriage.

Good marriages are based on principles found in the Word of God. Our problem is that we usually feed our minds more with the world's input than with God's. Garbage in, garbage out. If we spend more time filling our minds with the unrealistic secular versions of marriage, then we set ourselves up for failure through unrealistic expectation. If we continually remind ourselves of God's principles—let them dominate our thinking on marriage—we are on the road to making it work.

Marriage works when both the husband and wife make it work. Paul begins his instructions to husbands and wives with the mutual admonition: "Submit to one another out of reverence for Christ" (Eph. 5:21). Mutual submission, respect, selfless love, honor, purity, faithfulness, and servitude to one another are biblical qualities that make a marriage last. We must build our relationships and families on God's design, not Hollywood's dream. Unfortunately, what He has to say about it is heard less and less these days, as the divorce rate climbs.

2. *Buck the statistics: decide to make marriage last.* When my wife and I were married in 1975, we determined then and there that divorce would not be in our vocabulary. Fortunately, we both come from strong families with stable marriages, so we had good role models.

Dr. James Dobson surveyed 600 couples that had been married successfully for a number of years and discovered three fundamental principles that made these marriages last. Here are the three tried-and-tested recommendations:

• The family deeply committed to Jesus Christ has enormous advantages over the family with no spiritual dimension.
• No matter how much conflict or emotional blandness you generate at times, nothing short of death must ever

91

be permitted to come between you. A marriage will never last that begins with this vow: "I will stay with you for as long as I shall love you."

• A good marriage is not one where perfection reigns but where the partners talk things out. The needs of each partner must be communicated and understood by the other (1987:2).

Too many people are simply throwing their marriages on the junk heap because they don't know how to get the major repairs and overhauls they need to keep their relationships running. And boomers are guiltiest of all in this, not having the patience to work things out. If we want to make an impact (be salty) on the peers around us, there is probably no more crying need than for new hope in this arena of marriage. I appreciate Dobson's remark that the Christian marriage is not a place "where perfection reigns." People are not looking for perfect marriages, but marriages that keep working. Make your marriage last. If it is in trouble, get help. If it is not, keep growing so it doesn't get into trouble.

3. *Learn about role negotiations.* An important lesson Donna and I have learned is that our roles in marriage change during different periods of our lives. When we both worked outside the home, we had a certain way of splitting up household responsibilities that changed when she quit her job. Every time there is a major change in life, there has to be a fresh look at roles. For example, as each child comes along and as they change from infants to toddlers to teenagers, the needs in the family change, and husband and wife have to adjust.

It is natural for me to want to act the role in my home that my father played in our home when I was growing up. Tension comes when my wife naturally expects me to act like her father acted in their home. Maybe in her home Mom balanced the checkbook, but in my home Dad did it.

We must carefully discuss and negotiate who does what in *our* marriage, not only once but often throughout married life as circumstances change. The biggest mistake a husband or wife can make is to burden a spouse with unrealistic role expectations that have not been carefully and forthrightly discussed.

4. *Schedule regular meetings of the board of directors.* A time for communication must be planned. A successful marriage is like an elegant ship sailing through the waters and storms of life. The problem with all ships is that they get barnacles—ugly little unseen monsters that attach themselves to the bottom of the boat. Soon the vessel is stuck dead in the water—like the marriage that is going nowhere as the partners peacefully coexist. Little things, like the irritations of misunderstanding that come with wrong expectations, build up.

My marriage to Donna is a partnership, with the two of us responsible as the board of directors for the life of our family. Occasionally, we have to get away alone, to regroup and discuss the little irritations and expectations that have not been met. We get away to perform delicate loving surgery on one another, removing those ugly barnacles so our marriage is back up to speed. This is not always easy, and it doesn't always work smoothly, but it must happen.

5. *Women: if you can stay home, stay home!* Although I tread lightly on the issue, my personal conviction is that a woman's first priority is in the home when the children are young and not in school. If family members can make sacrifices and manage without her income, they should do it. More than anyone else, it is up to the husband to make that happen. If a wife and mother feels, before God, that her place is at home with her children, then that is where she belongs. I also hasten to add that she needs encouragement and support in this most vital work of preparing the next generation.

I *highly* recommend that all mothers who want to stay

home, or have already done so, read the excellent book *What's a Smart Woman Like You Doing at Home?* written by three aggressive homemakers, Linda Burton, Janet Dittmer, and Cheri Loveless (1986: Acropolis Books, Washington, D.C.). These three creative women have founded a fascinating new organization to support stay-at-home mothers: Welcome Home. A monthly newsletter they produce gives advice to the millions of women across America who are choosing to stay home. They contend that a new baby-boom mother is emerging in the 80s and 90s—not the housewife of the 50s or the working mother of the 70s—but a woman who puts her family first without putting herself last.

One alternative for many families today is *homespun businesses.* One of the creative ways that women are coping with the need to work but the desire to stay home is to run their own businesses out of their homes. There are 350,000 home-operated businesses in the United States owned and operated by women today. By 1990, there will be an estimated 500,000. These home-operated businesses are no light matter but are creating serious income for baby-boomer families. They run the gamut from services like nurseries and caterers to home-product sales, makeup, computer programming, real estate, architectural design, and even manufacturing consulting.

There is, of course, the problem of the millions of single-parent homes where the woman *must* work to care for her children, and we will look at meeting some of those challenges in chapter 10, "Living as a Single Baby Boomer."

Without a doubt, marriages are under fire today. Sadly, many married baby boomers, used to 30-minute TV solutions to all life's problems, would rather switch partners than work out problems in an existing marriage. This attitude toward the institution of marriage fosters all sorts of spin-off problems in American society today.

Here is a clear arena in which we can be salt. Christians

have a tremendous opportunity to glorify God through a marriage that shines amid the gloom of the modern-day marriage mess.

Thinking It Through

1. In what ways does today's world quietly battle against boomer couples as they attempt to maintain healthy relationships with each other and their children?

2. Think back to how your family divided the various household duties, how conflict was resolved, the role of finances, etc. In light of how things were in your family when you were growing up, what expectations do you bring into your marriage?

3. Describe what you have done or are now doing to cultivate the commitment to marriage and the relationship with your spouse. What else might you do to see your marriage grow in intimacy?

9

What about Our Kids?

"You'd never recognize dear old dad!"
Bronstein and Cowen, authors of *Fatherhood Today*

Have you noticed lately how many babies and young children there are? We baby boomers are having our own boomer boom.

I was working at a picnic table in a park near our home recently, trying to do some thinking and writing in a quiet, reflective atmosphere. All of a sudden, I heard an ominous roar. As I looked to see what all the noise was, I spotted an invading army of toddlers arriving on their big wheels. There must have been 50 kids, all between the ages of one and five, coming to enjoy the park with their baby-boomer moms. My quiet park! What a vivid reminder that was of the growing ranks of baby boomers with young families.

We are seeing a boomer boom all across the land. In an article entitled, "Making Way for the New Generation," Theresa Forsman documents the rising birthrate among boomers. According to her figures, there are now more children under five in the country than at any time in the last twenty years. The Census Bureau has named this newest generation—whose numbers are expected to peak in the 1990s—the *baby echo* period. Grade schools are beginning to see the first increase in enrollment in 15 years; preschools and nurseries are overcrowded. Hospitals are reporting a 25 percent increase in births between 1976 and 1986 (Forsman 1987:8).

Boomer babies have even made their presence known in the media. Little ones have suddenly become stars in popular TV shows and movies.

Conurturing Our Children

Cartoonist Gary Trudeau has been one of the most popular chroniclers of the baby-boom generation with his famous comic strip Doonesbury. In one episode Rick is trying to help his wife bathe their son. "Hi! Can I help?" asks Rick as he sees his wife struggling with the kid in the tub.

"*Help?* No, you can't *help,*" replies his wife in disgust. "*Help* implies that caring for our child is basically *my* responsibility, and that you're doing me a favor. Go out and try again." Poor Rick leaves the bathroom, dejected with head hung low.

Then he returns to give it another try. "Hi! Can I *conurture?*"

"No," she replies. "You always get the floor wet" (Aug. 4, 1987).

Today things are vastly different than they were when our parents were raising us. For one thing, fathers are much more involved in raising the children and doing housework, and many mothers work outside the home. I often take the kids to school, and since the birth of our twins, Donna and I often rotate who cooks dinner and who cleans up the dishes. It is a rare night that I don't drop into bed exhausted after another evening of conurturing.

During the day, Donna and I both work—I work outside the home and she works inside—so in the evenings we share the work of the family. I suppose we have come to feel like many couples do today, that raising our children is a joint effort between two equal partners in the project. Aside from the question of who has more energy in the evening, my children need me to be involved in their lives during the few hours I see them each week. One researcher reports that one third of the fathers in our generation are totally involved in the chores and work of raising their families—a dramatic rise from our parents' generation where Mom did most of the child rearing. That is a good trend.

Changing Family Values

In the 1990s, baby-boomer families will be vastly different from the families they grew up in during the 1950s. Boomer families will include stepchildren and second marriages and all sorts of custody arrangements. Not long ago my son Mark came home from kindergarten with a funny story to tell me about what had happened on the playground. It reminded me again just how much times have changed since I was a kid. One of his buddies had found a penny on the ground and decided he didn't want it, so he said to my six-year-old, "Here, Mark, take this home to your daddy—if you have a daddy."

Times are hard for many children as they see the security blanket of their parents ripped apart.

What about the Christian family? Christian parents are often fighting an uphill battle against the secular trends in family values today. Just last night my wife came home from a mother-of-twins meeting with another example of secular values. Each month the club has a different speaker, and this particular month the speaker was an expert in sibling rivalry, with a Ph.D. in psychology. He told this group of 100 young mothers that the keys to effective parenting are *hypnosis* and *discipline avoidance*. Hypnosis is to help the parents relax, and discipline avoidance is to keep the children from being stunted in their development.

This man encouraged parents not to discipline children

for anything because they only misbehave to get attention; therefore, discipline reinforces their negative behavior. He stated that someday America will be like Sweden, a nation that has abolished all forms of child discipline. I was disgusted. God forbid that America would follow after Sweden, where the divorce rate is *four times* that of the U.S., where living together is the norm for young couples, and where much of the world's child pornography is produced.

To be sure, baby-boomer Christians committed to raising young families in the late twentieth century are facing major pressures. The following list of positive and negative influences summarizes some of the major changes in the wind today:

Negative Forces:
* The demise of the nuclear family.
* The growing divorce rate and tremendous rise in the number of single-parent families.
* Different family mixes with stepdads and stepmoms, visiting boyfriends and girlfriends, all causing young children to wonder where they belong.
* Working mothers and 10 million children in day-care centers.
* Economic hardships on young families, especially in finding affordable housing.
* The general secularization of America, moving away from a biblical base for marriage and family.
* The unprecedented influence of modern TV, with its warped sitcoms, sex, and violence.
* Rising influence of peers as kids spend more time in day-care and after-school activities, and less time with parents.

Positive Forces:
* The proliferation of good teaching on marriage, child rearing, and family life.

- The back-to-home movement.
- The growing role of fathers in raising the children.
- The growing number of churches with excellent programs for families with young children.
- Partnership between husband and wife in the raising of the children.
- The Christian school movement.

Do We Raise Our Children Like Our Parents Raised Us?

The older I get, the more I see the cycles of life. When we were young, we felt a strong generation gap and thought our parents were "out of it." Now that we are older, and parents ourselves, we tend to be just like they were when they raised us.

As I get older, I can see my father's personality and mannerisms in me more and more. I'll say something to my kids or make a gesture and suddenly think, *That sounds just like what Dad used to say to me!* But in one area, I differ drastically from my father, and that is in how I relate to my children on an emotional and relational level.

When I was growing up, Dad worked from 8:00 A.M. until 4:30 P.M. He left for work every morning at 7:30 and walked in the door at 5:00 in the evening. Dad expected dinner on the table when he walked in the door, and he got it. Afterward, he sat down in his easy chair and watched the news while we helped Mom clean up. Yes, we even brought Dad his slippers!

I have never doubted my father's great love for me. He did so much for me, but in a way that was the problem in his generation. Many fathers showed their love for their children by providing *for* them, but often neglected being *with* them and getting to *know* them. Personal intimacy with parents has not been a strong element in the lives of most baby boomers.

It was very hard for me to talk to my father because he

never took the initiative. I frankly don't remember one intimate (as my generation defines the word) conversation I ever had with him . . . except the one that I forced on our relationship.

My father died a few years ago, but sweet memories of him remain strong in my mind and heart. What I remember most about him is our last conversation.

While working overseas in Vienna, Austria, we learned that my father was dying of cancer. We flew to be with him, knowing that it was just a matter of time before he would leave us. Finally, after a long visit, we had to get back to our work in Europe. The day before our final farewell, I decided I would do something I had never done before with him: I asked him to go out for coffee *just to talk*. Both of us knew that this was it—the final farewell in this life—but it was up to me to initiate the conversation if there was going to be any deep communion on this last sacred day.

As we sat over coffee in that restaurant in Indianapolis, I forced myself to be the initiator with my father. If I had not taken the initiative, that conversation never would have happened. It seems logical to me that the parent should always be the one with the greatest interest in keeping a close parent-child relationship, but that is often not the case. So I forced myself to ask my father a question that reached down to the issues of the heart: "Dad, how are you feeling about what is happening to you?" I listened quietly as my father began to talk honestly about his struggles and fears. How I cherished his words.

"Vati (German for dad)," I told him that afternoon, "I want you to know that I consider it a privilege to be your son. It is an honor for me to be the son of Alfred Finzel, and I want you to know that I will always proudly be your son, even when you're gone. And not only do I respect you, Vati," I said as tears welled up in both our eyes, "I love you. Never forget that." That hour over coffee was a sacred moment for us because our souls touched as never before.

That was the first, and unfortunately, the last time my father and I ever talked on that level because he died one month after our conversation. He left me with warm memories of that last cherished moment of intimacy.

I cannot forget my relationship with my father as I relate to my four children. Keeping in personal, intimate touch with the hearts of my three sons and sweet daughter is of *utmost* importance to me.

Parental Overkill: The Superkids Syndrome

In another Doonesbury cartoon, we are taken live to the Senate floor in Washington (Trudeau, Nov. 1, 1987):

Chairman: Mr. Secretary, forgive me for interrupting your testimony, but it's approaching 3:30, and I have to leave for my son's football game.

Mr. Secretary: I certainly understand, Mr. Chairman. I have two small children waiting for me myself.

Another Senator: As do I, Mr. Chairman. I'll have to excuse myself as well. I'm looking at a three-hour commute to get to my daughter's piano recital.

Chairman: Will the gentlemen yield?

Mr. Secretary: Of course, Senator.

Yet another Senator: Mr. Chairman, I, too, need to be excused. I've decided to leave public life altogether in order to spend more time with my family.

Chairman: Good luck to you, Senator. Okay, all those with family commitments are excused from the proceedings today . . . will those with messed up priorities please turn off the lights?

Before we leave the subject of boomers and their kids, I must speak to the issue of parental overkill that is a growing problem in our generation. Baby-boomer parents can become obsessive about their children. *Time* magazine reported this trend:

> Romanticizing their little creations, they have scorned traditional names like Bob and Mary Sue in favor of more precious monikers like Justin and Kimberly. Keenly aware of the terrible competition that they had faced for college admission and jobs, Baby Boomer parents often start their children on absurdly premature cram courses for the college boards, turning out pint-size superachievers stuffed with scientific nostrums and violin lessons.
> It would be no small irony, of course, if their children respond to the pressure by turning into the adolescent rebels—just like their parents (Thomas 1986:36).

Some parents are simply pushing their children too hard, not allowing them to enjoy the simple pleasures of childhood. Buzzwords among mothers, some trying to compete through their children, are *enrichment, stimulation* and *head start*. People are willing to pay thousands of dollars to put their children in high-pressure programs, some with uniforms and all, to make their little ones get the jump on their generation.

Preschool-age children are being forced into reading programs and other academic pressures that used to wait until grade school. Toys-R-Us has a whole major section of its stores set aside for academic games and computers for kids. Bookstores report that activity workbooks like *Fraction Action* and *See a Word, Say a Word* used to be purchased only by schools ten years ago. Now, parents gobble them up, especially before the summer holidays for summer tutoring. One publisher reports that workbooks for pre-schoolers are selling so fast that they can't print them fast enough. "These people are terribly success-oriented, but they don't realize that *any* good books are educational," says Judy Sarick, owner of The Children's Bookstore in Toronto. "One parent actually asked me for an encyclopedia for a 2-year-old" (Maynard 1984:195).

One survey I read asked parents in 1980 which quality they most desired in their children. *Intelligence* topped the list, followed closely by *personality*, then *creativity*, and *imagination* (Maynard 1984:194). What ever happened to trust, love, faith, honesty, and self-confidence? Aren't those the real building blocks for maturity?

What Should Be Different about Christian Parents?

As Christian parents, we must be careful not to let current baby-boomer values shape our thinking about raising children. Consider the following suggestions:

1. *We Christian parents should not allow society to push our children too fast.* Let's give them time to enjoy the normal joys of childhood. That worked for us—and other generations—and it will work for our children. Too many parents today expect too much from their children and try to compete with their peers through their children.

Children are forced to grow up too fast. They should instead be allowed to enjoy the simple life of play at home as long as possible. I remember spending lazy afternoons as a child playing cowboys and Indians or cops and robbers after school. Or we would play ball or get dirty in the backyard, digging for bugs. But now kids are so busy at such an early age. They rarely have time to be kids anymore.

Those parents who choose to keep their kids at home until first grade, or even homeschool them, sometimes worry about whether they will fall behind or be socially underdeveloped. There is plenty of evidence that proves neither is the case. In fact, kids that stay home longer usually do better than kids raised in day-care centers because they have developed better self-confidence and biblical values. We have chosen to keep our kids home until kindergarten, but we're not worried about their academic development. Our rationale is that God intended for children to be at home when they are little; they need love, security, warmth, and protection—not a head crammed full of knowledge and skills by age four!

In His childhood years, our Lord Jesus grew in wisdom and stature, and in favor with God and man. But we hear nothing of His childhood, other than that one time when He came out of obscurity to visit the temple. Then He goes back into seclusion until His ministry begins at age thirty.

I conclude, arguing out of silence, that His earthly parents and His Heavenly Father allowed Him to be a kid. He learned the lessons all children must learn in the quietness of His home with Mary and Joseph. He no doubt learned to work hard by doing chores. Eventually, He became a carpenter by trade. He certainly had few enrichment courses growing up in tiny Nazareth. I imagine His parents had all that they needed to raise Him right—with love, care, and discipline—in a God-fearing home that was built on biblical principles of wisdom.

2. *Our children, especially in their early years, need to know we love them.* Our love and personal attention create in them the trust and self-worth they will need to face the world later. Childhood expert Dr. Leo Lazer says that what children need most is to feel accepted and loved (Maynard 1984:202).

Being a father of four myself, I am very concerned with the impact I have on my little ones. One way I try to learn how to do the job right is to poll effective fathers. I have taken a private survey of fathers whose children have turned out the way I want mine to turn out. Though the words are always different, there is a strong common theme in all their comments: "Spend more time with your children."

Parents always seem to think that there will be more time for the children later, in a few months or years, but there never is. My own father is gone now, but I still think about him often, especially the times I spent *with him*.

3. *Our children need us to talk to them, listen to them, and just be with them*. My kids need me to talk to them, listen to them, and be available as part of their little world. My kids need me to play with them—something I try hard to do though it takes work on my part. They *don't* need things, and at early ages they don't need to be crammed full of knowledge and skills.

I'll never forget the words of advice from my own father as we were having our first baby: "Hans, it's easy to make children but hard to raise them right."

At times raising children right may require saying no in our careers. I can think of many times when I have had to do less than I could have done in my work for the sake of my family at home. I am not advocating irresponsibility at work; I am promoting putting family before career. In the pressure cooker of competition in many jobs, there is just more demanded of people than they have time to do. It is at those times that fathers and mothers may have to just say no—no to going the extra mile at work so they can walk the extra mile with their children. It may just be that the advances in our careers need to wait until the children are older. One piece of advice I heard sums it up well: "You'd better go fishing with your son today, or you'll go hunting for him tomorrow."

Some parents are naive enough to think that it is not *quantity* but *quality* time that counts. But children don't work that way and need us often when it is not our planned time to be with them.

Fortunately, many fathers are increasingly getting involved in the lives of their children—far beyond the traditional ball-tossing and coaching Little League. One idea I picked up from a friend is the practice of taking one of my children with me whenever I go on errands or short trips. It is more hassle for me, but it is such a joy for them to see Dad as he goes through the chores of his life. They need to enter into our world as much as we try to understand theirs. Our sons and daughters need Dad and Mom to read to them, pray with them, bathe and feed them (if they're little enough), enter into the world of their hobbies and interests, and willingly care for their physical, emotional, and spiritual needs.

Our children need *us* more than any material goods we can provide for them through our work. The more we rub shoulders with them in the nitty-gritty of life, the more our lives will be bonded to theirs, laying a solid foundation for their future.

4. *As we nurture our children, we must consider their uniqueness.* In an article entitled "Are Baby Boom Mothers Pushing Their Kids Too Hard?" Rona Maynard offers this conclusion to fight the problem of the superkid syndrome:

> Ultimately, the superkid mystique hurts all children and parents. It reduces childrearing, that most delicate and multifaceted of skills, to the search for absolutes: the right paraphernalia, the best program, the infallible performance-boosting techniques. It denies the uniqueness of every child and the right of every young person to shape a future that reflects personal goals—not simply parental ones (1984:202).

We need to let kids be kids and be unique. I don't want to push my children but to nurture them. "Fathers," Paul writes, "do not embitter your children, or they will become discouraged" (Col. 3:21).

I view children as tender young plants in need of the nurturing food, water, and sunlight that we as parents can provide for them in a home filled with love, honesty, trust, and encouragement. As they rise out of the soil of our family, we will begin to see what sort of plants they are. As I watch our four plants sprout, I see that some grow quickly and some take it slow, like the difference between squash and an oak tree. Some will be tall and some may be short. Some will produce fruit and others flowers. What they become and how they produce in life is basically up to them; our job is to nurture their young lives in the secure garden of our home with the values of love, honesty, truth, grace, and forgiveness.

5. *Children will thrive in a stable home.* Experts agree that what children need most is the quiet, protective, warm, and loving environment of a stable home where Mom and Dad love each other and love them unconditionally.

What do our children need most from us? The greatest thing I can do for my four kids is to love their mother. What that communicates to them is stability, security, protection, a feeling that everything is fine in our home because Mommy and Daddy are one. Break that unity and children fall apart emotionally and psychologically. We are kidding ourselves if we think it will work to ignore a rocky relationship with a spouse and focus only on our children.

I placed this chapter on children after the one on marriage for a purpose. The one lays the foundation for the other. The better the marriage, the more stable the children. Children in many ways become the sum total of what they absorb from the environment in which they grow up. An unknown writer sums it up well:

If a child lives with criticism, he learns to condemn.
If a child lives with hostility, she learns to fight.
If a child lives with fear, he learns to be apprehensive.
If a child lives with jealousy, she learns to feel guilty.
But,
If a child lives with encouragement, he learns to be self-confident.
If a child lives with tolerance, she learns to be patient.

If a child lives with praise, he learns to be appreciative.
If a child lives with acceptance, she learns to love.
If a child lives with approval, he learns to like himself.
If a child lives with honesty, she learns what truth is.
If a child lives with love, he learns that the world is a wonderful place to live in.

My greatest concern for baby-boomer parents is that they are too busy. Families are so busy with activities, plans, and programs that there is little time left for those quiet moments of family togetherness. How can values be transmitted if we never see each other? Who will teach our children the values they take with them into adulthood? The teacher? The coach? The baby-sitters? The day-care staff? The Sunday School worker? Their peers?

I often ask myself the question, "When my short time with them is done, what mark will I have left on my children?" It reminds me of the moving words of Abraham Lincoln: "A child is a person who is going to carry on what you have started. He is going to sit where you are sitting, and when you are gone, attend to those things which you think are important" (source unknown). What will I have communicated by my actions, as truly important?

Thinking It Through

1. Consider the ways parenting today might be different from the way it was in the 50s and 60s. List five positive changes and five negative changes you feel have taken place in the last 30 years.

2. Much was said in this chapter concerning the expectations boomer-parents are putting on their children, called the super-kid syndrome by some. In your opinion, is this a healthy or unhealthy trend? Why do you think so?

3. There has been an ongoing debate as to which is more

important to spend with your kids: quantity time or quality time. The author's point is that parents must get involved in the lives of their kids. What have you done to get involved? Describe what else you can do to keep in touch with your kids.

10

Living as a Single Baby Boomer

"Many people spend their entire lives indefinitely preparing to live."
—Paul Tournier

Author's Note: Many of you reading this book are single baby boomers. And you have unique needs and values that must be discussed in a book like this. When it comes to discussing singleness, I am definitely out of my league. I might be called married to a fault, 14 years into a delightful marriage with four wonderful but demanding children. And like most married couples, Donna and I are surrounded by friends whose lives are also full of the things that married people fill their time with.

So, I have called on my good friend Scott Last to write this chapter. He doesn't have his head buried in the sand on this important issue. His thoughts on the values and needs of single baby boomers are the result of eight years of effective ministry as singles pastor at Emmanuel Faith Community Church in Escondido, California.

****

Living alone has some great benefits. You only have to clean up before you know someone is coming over. Eating out costs a lot less. When you come home from a hard day's work, you can pamper yourself with a hot bath, the newspaper, music, or TV without anyone bugging you or expecting something from you. When you want to go somewhere, the only one you have to ask permission from is yourself. You are free to do as you please without anyone, except the law and your own limitations, to hold you back.

Sounds great, doesn't it? If "happiness is being single," why are most singles from the baby-boom era still searching for that special someone?

The media tell singles that they will find that special someone in a bar, sipping a Lite Beer. The media also promotes the notion that sex = intimacy, or at least that intimacy cannot be achieved without it.

How does a Christian single cope with this hunger for intimacy? Is there a way to celebrate solo living without having to face the mornings after? Can unmarried people actually experience intimacy without immorality? In other words, is the biblical concept of abundant living compatible with the single lifestyle, or is the Bible just too limited in scope to deal with the complex problems of singles today? These are some of the questions this chapter addresses.

Single Baby Boomers: Who Are They?

Let's begin by taking a look at some of the astounding facts and figures about our generation.

In 1976 a life insurance survey of young people born between 1951 and 1962 showed that only 32 percent of the respondents felt that marriage was a "great thing." Eighteen percent recommended that people should seriously consider remaining unmarried. However, baby boomers changed their attitude about marriage with age. Today, more than 9 out of 10 baby boomer men and women believe that marriage is the best lifestyle (Russell 1987:91-92).

But even though our generation has a renewed belief in marriage, more than half of baby-boomer marriages will end in divorce. Demographer Paul Glick explains: "Looking back on their lives, this is what baby boomers will see: 90% will have married once; half will have divorced once. One in three will have married twice, and one in five will have divorced twice. Five percent of baby boomers will have divorced three times" (Russell 1987:95).

The love-hate relationship baby boomers have with marriage is extraordinary. They think marriage is great; it's just their partner they don't like.

SINGLE PARENTS

Baby-boom couples are having significantly fewer children than their parents had. But each year the parents of over 1 million children divorce. Today, we have some 7 million Americans, 90 percent of whom are women, raising children alone. Half of these single parents have children under age six, and their median income is just one third of the median income of married couples with children (Russell 1987:105). (Upon divorce, a woman's income is usually reduced to 70 percent of its predivorce level, whereas a man's standard of living tends to increase.) This means that a whole class of struggling single mothers has been handed greater responsibility without resources to match. Many of them are not being helped by their ex-husbands and are forced to look to social services or the church just to get by. On the other hand, millions of formerly married men have fewer responsibilities, more money, and more time to do a great deal more than just merely survive.

The single parent world is not simply limited to those who have been divorced. Since Americans are no longer outraged at out-of-wedlock births, the number of older single women having children has risen dramatically. In fact, 65 percent of out-of-wedlock babies are born to women aged 20 and above. Twenty-nine percent are born to women aged 25 and older, and 11 percent are born to women 30 and above. It is significant that in a survey of single American women, 21 percent of the never-married respondents had children (Barna 1987:73).

THE NOT-YET-MARRIEDS

Last but not least, we have that group of singles who have never been married. As in previous generations, the number of singles who has never been married still make up the largest part of the singles population.

For the most part, this group tends to be careful about entering commitments too hastily. They cherish their freedom, and many of them are working hard to develop their careers. The thought of marriage is frightening because of the responsibility it involves and the chance of divorce. Yet, in our singles group these people don't really like being called "never-marrieds" much less "singles." Bert says, "Never-married sounds so permanent. I think not-yet married sounds much more like it." I couldn't have said it any better.

Some single boomers who believe in marriage but have trouble with lasting commitment and the conflicts that come with it are testing these treacherous waters in advance by living together. As of 1986, over 2 million households were counted in this category.

Intimacy

In its 1987 national survey of single adults, the Barna Research Group (Barna 1987:60) discovered that the life priority mentioned by 70 percent of singles from nearly all walks of life was "investing time and effort in close friendships." Fifty-five percent of the respondents stated that they valued "a growing relationship with Jesus Christ." As surprised as I was by the second statistic, combined with the first one, it only further confirmed what I had suspected for a long time. Single adults are in search of meaningful personal relationships—with others and with God.

Despite popular opinions to the contrary, most singles are not hooked on pleasure-seeking pursuits simply to satisfy their hedonistic desires. In fact, the image of the "swinging single" is a grossly exaggerated stereotype. Many of the unmarried are so busy with their jobs, children, and other responsibilities that they don't have time to live a "swinging" lifestyle, even if they could afford to.

Still, as the song says, some single baby boomers are "lookin' for love in all the wrong places." Others, meanwhile, are conducting their search for intimacy in "healthier" environments like recreational or social clubs or even church groups, like ours. The environment in which the search is carried out does make a difference, but it is also true that many bad relationships do come out of "good environments."

For example, consider this relationship pattern that I have seen all too often. The names change but the actions are the same. Brenda meets Frank at a social function. Both are still trying to get over the pain of their previous relationships and rejections. They begin to talk and find that they have some things in common. They are tired of being lonely. There is an immediate attraction between them. They go out for coffee afterward. Starting the next day, I never see one without the other. Then, after a few weeks or months, Frank suddenly pulls back. Something has suddenly changed, and he just wants to be friends. She is devastated.

The above is just a typical example of a relationship pattern with many possible scenarios. Sometimes the roles are reversed. Sometimes the relationship goes on and on for years in an "on-again-off-again" kind of way. Sometimes the man and woman involved get married, only to break up in the first year or two. Occasionally, they make it through the obstacles and have a good marriage. But, in my experience, relationships that start this way seldom last, at least not without some major, midstream changes being made. The problem has to do with the fact that romantic feelings arise quickly and are mistakenly equated with true intimacy. Thus, the couple becomes too close, too soon. In the process, they are unwittingly sabotaging their chances for intimacy by practicing intimate behavior before its time.

This is love, American-style. This is the way most of our culture chooses to play the dating game. It is reinforced in countless romantic novels, TV episodes, and movie plots. This romantic model looks so exciting and good on the screen: intimacy achieved in one hour or less (depending on the length of the show). It's too bad that such a beautiful looking model has to have a hidden flaw. It simply doesn't work.

Why not? The biggest reason, in my opinion, comes from a fundamental error in understanding what intimacy is all about. In our lifetime we have seen more accomplished in shorter periods of time than our ancestors ever dreamed possible. We have come to expect almost instant answers to previously unsolvable problems. The solution to any dilemma seems to lie in our ability to manufacture it, fix it quickly, or throw it away and buy a new one. This is fine when it comes to achievement in the material world. But it doesn't work with relationships. As Terry Hershey says it so well in his book, *Intimacy:* "Intimacy is not a destination or a possession or a status. Intimacy is a journey" (1984:18).

If this is true, then we can expect to see rushed relationships burn out quickly. There are no shortcuts to intimacy precisely because it is not a destination to be reached. Intimacy cannot be processed or possessed, microwaved or manufactured.

Intimacy is not achieved through sex or emotional excitement. In fact, sex without genuine commitment produces insecurity because of how it raises relationship expectations without any guarantees of fulfillment. No wonder the Bible prohibits sex outside of marriage (1 Cor. 6:12-20). It is for the protection of His people against the emotional hurts it can cause. I have counseled many people who became sexually involved outside of marriage only to experience great personal hurt and the death of their relationship.

Intimacy is founded on trust, which is earned over the long haul and reaffirmed daily. Those who try to build an intimate relationship on attraction, romance, and body chemistry at the expense of work, self-sacrifice, and self-control are just not in touch with what the journey is all about. They have set themselves up for disappointment. Disneyland is a wonderful place to visit, but real life and real relationships aren't built there.

The harder we search for intimacy, the less likely we are to find it. This is a frustrating principle for single baby boomers. This is true in male-female relationships, and in same-sex friendships. Patty is a girl who always seems to be changing best friends. "What is it about her that drove you away?" I asked one of her former friends.

"It was great at first. She really is a wonderful person. It's just that she is so intense and expects so much from me. I was being smothered by her desire for intimacy." Intimacy cannot be created instantly. It comes as a by-product of living an unselfish, loving kind of life. It is a gift that is given only to those who are willing to give up their right to it by putting the needs of others ahead of their own.

Today's pop psychology says that you have to love yourself before you can love others. There's an element of truth to this since God commands us to "love your neighbor as yourself" (Lev. 19:18). But the command focuses on loving our neighbor. It assumes that we already love ourselves enough. All of us are basically self-centered creatures. So the last thing we need to be told is to love ourselves more. This only drives us more inward, increases our selfishness, and blocks our potential for intimacy. Instead, we need to realize that a relationship with God is the basis for loving relationships with others. "We love because He first loved us" (1 John 4:19). Then as we let the Author of Love show us how love really works, and put our own ideas and selfishness out of the way, we will find that intimacy will become a regular part of our lives.

The study of intimacy is a fascinating one. It deserves much more space than I have here. For more complete coverage of the subject I recommend two books: *Intimacy*, by Terry Hershey (Merit Books:1984) and *Too Close, Too Soon* by Jim Talley and Bobbie Reed (Thomas Nelson:1982). These offer tremendous insights into understanding and developing healthy relationships.

Freedom

While it is true that most singles are interested in building intimate relationships, at the same time they are very protective of their freedom. This is especially true of the single without the responsibility of raising children. How ironic that the very thing so many singles want desperately, intimacy, represents such a threat to their most treasured possession: freedom. Nevertheless, in the world of single baby boomers, so many are trying to have both. "Who says you can't have it all?" says a popular commercial. And a significant number of singles are going for it, especially the males.

George is a good example of the man who wants to have it all. He has a great paying job in the high tech industry. He owns a nice home, a sports car, an economy car, and a motorcycle. He has all the other "necessary" trinkets and material status symbols of our day. He looks good, stays in shape, plays and works hard, enjoys travel, and has a woman who really cares for him. He is about to lose this woman, though, just like he has lost other women before. He is 35 years old, yet he insists, "The marriage commitment is not for me. I couldn't handle the responsibility."

George is a worshiper at the shrine of freedom. I give him credit for knowing it. Most freedom-seekers don't realize how self-centered they are until they get into trouble by making commitments they can't keep. Freedom for George means that the most important priority of his life is himself and his own happiness. All other needs take a backseat to his own. Thus, he has learned to manipulate others very effectively to give him what he wants (until they finally see through him and say good-bye).

The problem with George, however, is that he is really insecure and alone. He is a high-wire artist without a net. He is a self-sufficient "lone ranger" without backup in case of an emergency. He goes on with his present course of life because his inner pain does not yet outweigh his hope that somehow, someway he will be able to find a woman he can keep without having to make a commitment to her. His thinking, like the thinking of so many other singles, is that he can get what he wants without really having to give anything back.

The trouble with this kind of thinking is that it is not in tune with the way life really is. God has set up His creation with certain laws and limitations that cannot be violated without consequences. A farmer will never have a harvest if he doesn't plant. Gravity must be respected. People can't live underwater without air. Love and friendship can't exist without sacrifice and commitment.

Most singles I know are not as openly committed to freedom as George. Their attitudes and actions are usually much more subtle. Many of them talk about how they desire to be more giving and committed to God, to ministry, or to others. But so often, when a specific opportunity is given them to demonstrate their commitment, such as reaching out to someone in need or just helping out in a project, most will stay away in droves. That is, unless the event somehow becomes an attractive social happening with all the right people there.

In the final analysis, I feel that the freedom-seeking baby boomer has often ended up exchanging the real thing for a caricature. A great number of us in our pursuit of freedom have discovered selfishness instead. Bob Dylan wrote a song a few years back that says, "Everybody's got to serve somebody." Many single boomers, who have no one to answer to but themselves, have ended up becoming enslaved to themselves. This looks and feels like freedom because "self" is calling the shots. But from what does this kind of freedom set us free? It sets us free from the ability to expand beyond ourselves, to rely on the wisdom and power of God, and to enjoy the intimacy that comes from laying aside our own needs to meet those of another.

So often we have been led to believe that submitting to God and His commands is restrictive and limiting. In reality, just the opposite is true. God, as the all-wise Creator of the universe has revealed the secrets of how His creation works best in the principles and commands of Scripture. He tells us to abide by them so that we will be blessed, so that we will succeed, and so that we will not self-destruct.

The biblical teaching on divorce is a sticky area that many singles feel to be anti-freedom and repressive. Indeed, God says, "I hate divorce" (Mal. 2:16). Thus, it is commanded throughout Scripture that husbands and wives be faithful to one another and stick together even through the tough times. But so many of us have missed the point as to why God hates divorce. It is primarily because *God loves His people*. Divorce may offer freedom from a bad marriage, but it is always offset by great pain throughout the entire divorcing family. In my experience, I have never met a divorced person who likes divorce.

Fortunately, God offers love, healing, and forgiveness to divorced people. Divorce is not the unpardonable sin. But any divorced person will most likely admit that his or her divorce, even if permitted by Scripture (Matt. 19:9; 1 Cor. 7:15), has been a difficult ordeal. Singles who seek to be married or remarried would be wise to obtain the counsel of someone who knows the Bible and how it applies to family living situations.

God is on our side, looking after us. He simply knows what works and what doesn't, as any creator would know about his creation. No wonder Jesus says, "If you hold to My teaching, you are really My disciples. Then you will know the truth, and the truth will set you free" (John 8:31-32). True freedom is not found in autonomy; it is found in believing and practicing the truth revealed by God in the Bible.

Laura is a living example of this reality. She recently said to me, "For so long I have been afraid to really commit myself to God and to His will for me. But now that I am finally unstuck and involved in doing what He wants for me (even though some of it is very hard), I have never felt freer in my life!"

Purpose

The last issue of concern in this chapter is the single baby boomer's need for a sense of purpose. I have found that so many of them seem to live in a perpetual state of transition. Most seem to view their singleness as a temporary segment of their lives—a view which is statistically validated. But the problem that often develops from this perspective is a feeling that their lives are on hold until they get married. Psychologist Paul Tournier made the sad comment, "Many people spend their entire lives indefinitely preparing to live" (Hansel 1979:80). How true this is of so many singles who are simply drifting until their dreamboat comes along to give them a reason to let their life begin to sail.

I was listening to Diane one day as she told me how she had decided not to pursue a career opportunity. She had planned to be married and wanted to remain flexible for the sake of her husband. Now, as she approaches age 30 with no marriage prospects in sight, she feels more than a little foolish and resentful. By putting all her eggs in one basket she has kept herself from greater financial security and job satisfaction. What if she never gets married?

One of the most important ideas that I seek to communicate to single adults is that they can discover and fulfill their purpose in life whether or not they get married. In fact, their status offers them greater freedom and single-mindedness to develop and pursue that purpose.

If you are single, let me assure you that marriage is not the secret to discovering and unlocking your potential. Whether you are married or single, God has given you unique abilities and interests that you can use to bring joy to Him, others, and yourself. Here are some questions to ask yourself that can help you identify these abilities and interests so that you can develop them and put them to work in a truly meaningful way. What do I enjoy doing and do well? What do others say I am good at? How can I use my interests and abilities to please God? How can I use them to help others? With whom or with what organizations can I associate so as to make a more positive contribution? What are my needs and desires (spiritual, professional, physical, intellectual, emotional, etc.)? Am I taking steps to help in their fulfillment?

If you begin to start answering these questions now as a single, you can have a fulfilling and well-directed life regardless of your marital status. Then, as you confidently head on your life course, you will attract others who are going that same direction. Out of that group you are more likely to find the right marriage partner if that is what you desire.

Just one more thought in closing. Never underestimate the influence you can have as a single adult. Even though many in the couples world look at singles as misfits or lonely hearts, you and I know better. Some of the most courageous, creative, and inspiring people I know are single baby boomers like you.

The singles in our church continue to impact our whole community through active programs that feed and evangelize the homeless and help heal the hearts of those going through divorce. Singles teach our children, care for the elderly, and provide other vital leadership functions.

Your life can be rich and effective as a single adult. Don't forget that Jesus Christ and the Apostle Paul were single. They even taught that single living was preferred over marriage for those who could control their sexual feelings (Matt. 19:10-12; 1 Cor. 7). Your life and your potential is a special gift from God. For His sake and your own, don't waste it.

Thinking It Through

1. With the image painted for us by our peers and the media, we are easily deceived by the stereotype of the swinging single. In what ways is the swinging single a myth?

2. Singles are no different than anyone else in their need and desire for meaningful relationships. Consider a good friendship you have been in or now enjoy. What made the relationship special? How can your understanding of intimacy influence your relationships?

3. So often our understanding of terms and concepts are in conflict with what is actually correct. A case in point is found in the word *freedom*. This word brings to mind a wide range of emotions, memories, and experiences. Describe a time in your life when you had a poor understanding of freedom and another time when you better understood what it meant to be free.

11

Making a Difference inside America's Largest Generation

*"And he will be like a tree firmly planted
by streams of water"*
—Psalm 1:3.

Compared to the generations before us, we have suffered little and been spoiled much. And like a child that is sheltered and spoiled, we have in many ways prolonged our adolescence as a generation. It is no secret that many baby boomers postpone a lot of things, from career choice to marriage to parenthood.

It's true. Our generation doesn't always enjoy the thought of really growing up. The problem is that the postponing attitude among boomers has infected the Christian community at large. We too have been reluctant to pursue maturity, defined by deepened commitment on many fronts.

Christians need not one conversion but three, in order to make an impact in the world for Jesus Christ. First, they must be committed to the *person of Christ*. But it shouldn't stop there. Christians committed only to Christ can be very self-centered in our individualistic generation. That may sound strange, but our Lord Himself would agree. The second conversion is to the *people of Christ:* His church. Christians must develop a strong connection to the body of Christ. But even that is not enough. Christians with only those two conversions still tend to be focused inward. The third conversion is to the *passion of Christ:* reaching the world with the power of His love. Thrice-converted baby boomers will make a lasting impact on their generation.

Christian baby boomers who want to make a difference in their generation will have to make strong personal commitments that their peers will neither emulate nor appreciate. The pages of this final chapter will present three areas in which these commitments must operate—each vital in its own right and yet connected to the other: commitments of the heart, commitments in the church, and commitments to the world.

Commitments of the Heart

"Let me be taught," wrote Henry Martin, "that the first great business on earth is the sanctification of my own soul" (Wiersbe 1980:82). Somehow, our generation seems to have missed this truth from generations past.

Just this week I had lunch with a good friend who told me of conversations he has had with three pastors over the last several months. In each case, the man (a baby boomer) was eminently successful on the outside—a model pastor—yet lived in immorality in the darkness of his secret life. The sad thing is that we have a system today that allows that type of leadership to go on unnoticed. I call it the "character gap."

Where is our concern for character? Who is taking time for this great business of the sanctification of our souls? Why can the leaders of our generation be so flashy on the outside, yet so hollow on the inside?

This "character gap" represents the tension between the world's values and biblical Christianity. The greatest battle for the Christian baby boomer is to focus on internal issues of the heart while peers are pursuing externals with reckless abandon.

We need to stockpile lasting treasures in heaven and learn to ignore our peers who are building their castles of sand. As Christ said, "What good is it for a man to gain the whole world, yet forfeit his soul?" (Mark 8:36) In other words, "What good is it to be a Christian and forfeit all usefulness to Christ by pursuing selfish dreams?" Some people are deluded into thinking that both are possible.

Character is the issue we must begin with: *commitments of the heart*. My goal here is not to tell anyone *how* to go about developing character as much as to emphasize the *importance* of focusing on internals first in our lives. Our Christian bookstores are filled with good books on how to develop the inner soul; we just don't put a priority on it in our generation. We are long on *reading* but short on *doing*.

How do we develop the power of character? Not by any 60-second solution or "one minute manager." We must take some of the following medicine—hard for us to swallow, but necessary if we want the symptoms of superficiality to go away.

1. We must be *devoted* to the development of our personal character through relationship with Jesus Christ on a personal and regular basis.

Soon after my conversion in 1970, I discovered the fascinating world of Scripture memory. As an eager young convert I was hungry for the Word of God, and discovered that memorizing large portions of the Bible nourished me and changed me. I was taught by my mentors that the Bible would be used by the Holy Spirit to cleanse me from the sin patterns of my former life and renew me in the likeness of Christ. So I went to work! I had much that needed changing.

During those college days in the early 1970s, I drove a truck for a summer job. As I drove the backroads of northern Alabama in those months, God's Word filled my mind and changed my heart. God delivered me with great power from all kinds of ungodliness that I don't care to spell out. Though I was immediately a new creation in God's sight at my conversion (2 Cor. 5:17), I learned that the practical transformation of my character and lifestyle took time and needed the nourishment of the Scriptures (Ps. 119:9-11).

In some ways I miss those simpler days of my new life in Christ, days filled with rapid growth and constant spiritual discovery. It was during those truck-driving days that I memorized a passage of Scripture that expressed the heart and soul of what I wanted for my new life in Christ. It still means a great deal to me and forms the basis of my approach to living an alternative life amid the mixed-up values of my generation.

How blessed is the man who does not walk in the counsel
of the wicked,
Nor stand in the path of sinners,
Nor sit in the seat of scoffers!

But his delight is in the law of the Lord,
And in His law he meditates day and night.
And he will be like a tree firmly planted by streams of
water,
Which yields its fruit in its season,
And its leaf does not wither;
And in whatever he does, he prospers.

The wicked are not so,
But they are like the chaff which the wind drives away.
Therefore the wicked will not stand in the judgment,
Nor sinners in the assembly of the righteous.
For the Lord knows the way of the righteous,
But the way of the wicked will perish.

Psalm 1, NASB

I have copied the words of that psalm from the very Bible I carried in my truck during those long, hot Alabama summers. It was my very first Bible, a greater treasure now as each year goes by. Looking at the smeared and dirty pages, I realize that the dust, sweat, and grime came from my young, 19-year-old hands as I pored over those precious pages hour after hour. If I have had any success in my Christian life these last 20 years, it is because of the grace of God and the foundation that I began laying in those early days.

2. We must learn to *deny* ourselves by turning off the perpetual accumulation machine. God's Word reminds us:

Since, then, you have been raised with Christ, set your hearts on things above, where Christ is, seated at the right hand of God. Set your mind on things above, not on earthly things. For you have died, and your life is now hidden with Christ in God (Col. 3:1-4).

This speaks to one of the greatest battles of the baby boomers. *Newsweek* magazine claims that our generation has reached a new level of consciousness: *transendental acquisition* (Colsen 1985:19). Christians must buck this generational trend because it is just impossible to be devoted to the gods of hedonism and materialism and also fill our lives with the things of God.

One of my good friends recently demonstrated courage in this area in a mighty way—chalk up one victory for this baby boomer. He was working weekends to make extra money for his family yet finding little energy left for them or his church or for his own spiritual growth. Driving around in a ten-year-old car he was very tired of, he had his heart set on buying a new compact pickup truck. As we were enjoying a cup of coffee over breakfast he told me, "Hans, I finally decided it was stupid. Why work weekends away from my family just so I can get that truck—that's what it

131

boils down to, and I don't *need* it or the other things money
can buy as much as my family needs me." He stopped
working weekends. He made the decision in his context to
just say no. The change in his life in recent months is obvious to me. The result is more time for the things above, the
unseen things, the important things eternal.

3. We must *dare* to live as Christians in a world that will
reject us as it rejected Christ.

I have recently been stimulated by the writings of
Dietrich Bonhoeffer, a fellow German of whom I am proud
and a salty churchman during the reign of Hitler.
Bonhoeffer had the courage to be different and speak out
when most of the church in Germany remained silent during the Second World War. His courage finally cost him his
life. Hitler himself ordered Bonhoeffer's execution, sadly
only a few weeks before the war ended. Of course, God
could have changed the war timetable and spared this servant, but it was His design to have Bonhoeffer martyred for
the faith.

In his book, *Cost of Discipleship,* Bonhoeffer helps me to
see the important difference between suffering and rejection. Many people don't mind a little suffering, but no one
can stand rejection—especially the baby boomers.

Jesus said in Matthew 16:24 that "if anyone would come
after Me, he must deny himself and take up his cross and
follow Me." When speaking of these words of Christ,
Bonhoeffer sheds great light on their meaning, first in what
it meant for Christ Himself:

There is distinction here between suffering and rejection.
Had He only suffered, Jesus might still have been ap-
plauded as the Messiah. It could have been viewed as a
tragedy with its own intrinsic value, dignity and honor.
But his rejection robs the passion of its halo. It must be a
passion without honor. Suffering and rejection sum up
the whole cross of Jesus.

Now we followers of Christ must join in the pain of that terrible word "rejection," as Bonhoeffer goes on to explain:

> Just as Christ is Christ only in virtue of His suffering and rejection, so the disciple is a disciple only in so far as he shares his Lord's suffering and rejection and crucifixion. Discipleship means adherence to the person of Jesus, and therefore submission to the law of Christ which is the law of the cross (1959:95-96).

Sure, some of us might be willing to suffer a bit, but are we willing to be counted "out" of the mainstream and heartbeat of our generation?

But that is just the cost we are being asked to pay.

Commitments in the Church

If there is one collective weakness that stands out among Christian baby boomers I have observed, it is a general lack of commitment to the local church. Our hectic pace of life leaves little time for deep, personal relationships. Many of us, if we're honest, must admit a general lack of commitment today to anything outside of a very narrow personal orbit.

Yet for a believer to make it in the battle to be salt and light, there is no way around deep involvement in a local church. My life has *got* to touch the lives of others in intimacy and honesty. Community, not individuality, is God's pattern. The plain fact is that being in the community of Christ fans the flames of our spiritual passions, which easily go out when we are alone:

> And let us consider how we may spur one another on toward love and good deeds. Let us not give up meeting together, as some are in the habit of doing, but let us encourage one another—and all the more as you see the Day approaching (Heb. 10:24-25).

Our trouble is that we *meet* but we don't *spur;* we're there but we're not. We sit in the pew on Sundays often so exhausted from the busy week that it is really a time to rest and daydream and let our mind and soul catch up with our bodies. Very little energy is left to give to the church. We see the people at church on Sundays, but what do we *really* know about the hurts and joys of their lives? We may have the solutions to their needs, but we never get that far with them. Christ called us "parts" of His body, but how do we expect to function successfully as disjointed distanced members of one another? We must be committed to God's people in our churches if we are to be effective baby-boomer agents of change.

It is my conviction that every man and woman needs a sharpening friendship, even beyond the bond of a marriage partner. Through the years I have always tried to have at least one intimate friend with whom to be transparent and truthful about the struggles and joys of faith. These friends have made all the difference, especially in the times of deep despair and failure that plague us all from time to time. I need someone in the body of Christ that I can trust—someone to help hold me accountable to the goals and commitments I make to Christ from year to year:

> Two are better than one, because they have a good return for their work: If one falls down, his friend can help him up. But pity the man who falls and has no one to help him up! (Ecc. 4:9-10)

Commitments to the World

In the fall of 1969, the summer after Woodstock and the first manned moon landing, I joined half a million of my radical peers as we marched on the capitol in Washington, D.C. I can still remember that week. The agitation over the problems of the world that raged in many of our hearts during the '60s was coming to a boil. We wanted revolution, though we had no solutions—only complaints. We shouted *peace* and *love*—the catchwords of our generation—though we had neither. As we threw rocks at the riot police and marched toward the Justice Department, we chanted slogans like, "Two, four, six, eight; organize to smash the State!" Within two hours the police had managed to move all half a million of us into the Potomac and beyond, using brute force, tear gas, and massive arrests.

I look back on those days in amazement. What happened to that zealous concern for the ugly problems of the world that we used to have? Where is our social conscience today?

One of the exciting things that happened in those days was that many of us found a living faith in Jesus Christ for the first time. Suddenly, the fantasy Jesus of childhood Sunday School became the bigger-than-life man Jesus who could answer the big problems of our hearts. Many of us found Christ in those college years—the true revolutionary who could change the world by changing the hearts of men and women from the inside.

In the '60s we had no answers but many complaints. Today it seems that many of us have the answer in Jesus Christ but no complaints. There is a crying need for more of us to rekindle our concern for the needs of the world— especially the spiritual needs of a suffering humanity dying without Christ.

We have the chance in our generation to write the next chapter of church history. What will be said of our concern for the world? How will we be measured in terms of our commitment to reaching our generation for Christ? What will we have added to the church when we pass off the scene?

Not long ago I received a letter from some friends that illustrates well what I am driving at in terms of commitment. These older baby boomers felt the tug of the needs of the world on their heartstrings and decided to do something about it. Here is a part of that letter:

Lowell had worked for HP nearly 17 years, so it took a lot of time for the Lord to get us ready to make the break with secular work and get on with bigger and better things. It's amazing to think that we started to pray with two couples in 1976, asking the Lord to show us if it was His will for us to one day go into full-time service and, if so, where we were supposed to serve. Today, all three of us are in full-time work—some answer to prayer, huh?!

Not everyone is able to go into full-time, professional ministry like these three couples, but I can tell you truthfully that many more are desperately needed in all phases of Christian work. Everywhere that I travel or speak to friends who work overseas, I see personnel shortages. In many places the work of God is not going forward for lack of the two essentials: money and manpower. It is my observation that getting the money is easier than getting the lives. Many times I meet fellow baby boomers who say to me, "I wish I had made the choices you made when I was younger—your life seems to really count, and I feel trapped now." My advice to them is simple—it is never too late to get serious about serving Christ. Pray over it and ask Him how you can serve with small pieces of time, or part-time, maybe even full-time.

What God demands is that we all take an honest look at the needs around us and do something to meet those needs. The Apostle John put it well: "Dear children, let us not love with words or tongue but with actions and in truth" (1 John 3:18). It may be service in your church; it may be volunteer work in a counseling center, rescue mission or home for unwed mothers. Every church needs help in reaching out into the community with evangelistic efforts. Our hospitals and nursing homes are filled with lonely, hurting people who need words of comfort from those who know the God of all comfort. Often it is sacrifical use of your finances to help your church and those believers who are in full-time ministry. And for some of you, it will be the call of God on your lives to serve Him full-time in ministry. Heed that call whatever the cost—you'll never regret it.

We have finally come to the culmination of what the Christian life is all about—meeting the needs of the world. God has left us *in* the world that we might make an impact *upon* it. Somehow we have to ignite the sleeping passion that lies dormant in our generation and turn again to the concerns beyond ourselves. We have the resources, the manpower, the talents, education, and abilities. We lack only the passion.

Many in our generation have committed themselves to the work of Jesus Christ, but many more are needed. It is now up to us to take our turn to write the story of how the baby boomers reached their world for Jesus Christ.

Thinking It Through

1. When discussions of commitment come up with baby boomers, one often hears things like "But who has the time?" or "I really can't get into that anymore." It would appear commitments are hard for baby boomers to make. Do you agree or disagree?

2. Various commitments were discussed in this chapter. What kind of commitments do you feel you need to develop in order to make a positive impact in your sphere of influence?

3. Describe the things you would need to do as a lifelong practice in order to see that these commitments never drift into mere memories of a better time in your life. Who can you think of who would be willing to journey with you on this path of commitment? Write down when you will talk with this person about committing yourselves to making a difference, then do it.

Epilogue

How Churches Can Reach out to Baby Boomers

In the year that I have worked on the material for this book, I have had many long talks with pastors and church workers about my thoughts on baby boomers. The importance of churches understanding the baby boomers keeps popping up, so I felt it helpful to add these thoughts on how churches can reach out to the baby-boom bulge. These thoughts are directed especially at those of you who work in Christian organizations and churches on either a lay or professional level.

Harnessing a Vital Generation
What are our churches doing to meet the needs of our generation? Some might even say that such a question is a moot point—that churches don't need to cater to the whims of the moment. Not true. We are not talking about whims; we are talking about understanding a generation and building a bridge into their hearts.

Baby boomers need to be committed to the local church, but the church needs to be committed to baby boomers as well. One reason many of us are not as involved as we should be is that old structures are not meeting new needs.

Like a soldier who needs his platoon, baby boomers who seriously want to live lives of alternative values need the church to survive the battle. And churches that want to meet the needs of boomers must change some ways of doing things.

Reaching out to Baby Boomers

I feel that there are at least nine important pointers that churches need to keep in mind if they want to harvest and harness America's largest generation.

1. *Welcome back the baby boomers.* According to Benton Johnson, professor of sociology at the University of Oregon, our generation rejected Christianity and church-going on a scale "unprecedented in all of American history." But with the fast-paced 1980s and the pressure of increased competition in the workplace, many of our generation are feeling increasingly alone. We are a mobile, transient, and basically solo generation. In an article entitled "Dropping Back In," Ann Japenga of the LA Times says that a "growing number of baby boomers are discovering there's no place like church" (1988:IV;1).

While sociologists are still working to explain the trend, a major reason for reinhabitation of the pews is that baby boomers are finding that church feels like home. And many boomers are now finally settling down to building homes and families for the first time. The church is providing a sense of home and community in an increasingly impersonal world where people are looking for a place to belong. What this means is that churches should understand this tremendous trend and do all they can to welcome back this generation with open arms.

2. *Cultivate a sense of community.* In the complex world of the '80s and '90s, baby boomers need "body life" much more than they did in the '60s and '70s when Ray Stedman

first pioneered that movement. The fastest growing churches in America today recognize the essential need for small cell groups and place strong emphasis on getting the people of the pew involved in community and accountability.

New ways of getting us involved in such relationships need to be pioneered, and it is imperative that they be made workable in the different lifestyles of today's baby boomers.

3. *Promote accountability networks.* It is difficult to have deep friendships in the fast-tracking '80s and '90s. We are all so busy raising our families and building our careers that there is little time left in today's crowded lifestyles for intimate friendships. But those friendships are essential, as we saw in the last chapter. The church is a place where these networks can be built and encouraged. The leaders who structure the programs of the church should ask themselves if they are driving people close to each other or away from each other by the plans and schedules they promote. There is no greater need in our churches today than women's and men's discipleship networks.

4. *Be open to changes in your churches.* Recently I was invited to speak in a large, established church in Arizona. When the pastor met me at the airport, I was excited to learn he is a fellow baby boomer, not because I don't like older people, but because I enjoy seeing how a young, new pastor copes with the existing leadership which is a generation older. "How well is this newer-generation thinker doing in an old, established setting?" I asked myself.

Mark is my age, late thirties, and one year into the pastorate of a large church. Like many of our contemporaries, he stepped into the job of leadership, replacing someone older with more traditional ideas of how to run a church. I admire Mark's patience. He told me on the way home from the airport, as we were enjoying the beautiful desert mountains surrounding his town, that he is trying to go slow with making changes. "In this first year," he began, "I have tried to listen to my people and get a solid feel for the situation before I introduce any changes." His burden is to reach his city for Christ and to meet real needs with real solutions.

He shared with me his struggle as he wants to honestly evaluate every activity of the church to see if it is still valid for today. "It seems that so much of the activity of our church is no longer functional," he continued. "I don't want to spend all my time going to banquets and maintaining an institution while our city is in crying need of our Saviour."

My mind jumped to the issue of generational values, and I saw again how very different the generations are in the way they approach life—church life too. So far this church is allowing him to move in the direction of new wineskins, and I wish him well.

Mark—like most baby boomers—doesn't worship change for change's sake. If he did, he would be wrong. What he sees is a dire need for the church to speak and act in new ways to reach this massive new generation that is often untouched by the old, traditional methods. Sure, the basic needs of people never change, but how we approach them and package our message must change to meet them where they are today. The message of hope and new life in Jesus is sacred and unchanging; the method of delivery is not. That principle brings me to my next point.

5. *Hold traditions lightly*. Of course, we baby boomers are notorious for being tradition-smashers. For many of us it is a holdover from the spirit of the '60s, combined with a recognition of the radical changes of the *Third Wave* effecting our society. When a boomer walks into a church, he begins by asking the question, "Why are you doing what you're doing?" And the answer must make sense from the perspective of function, not tradition.

Most baby-boomer Christians don't seem to be attracted to the more traditional churches. They are responding more to the churches that are using forms more in step with the times. In an article, "Baby Boomers: Time to Pass the Torch?" Jack Sims points out a number of reasons why baby boomers are turned off to more traditional churches:

- Because we are individualistic, and shy away from the rigid structure we see in most churches.
- Because of different tastes in music.
- Because baby boomers find their experiences with church and the religious media to be boring, irrelevant, or high-pressured.
- Because they are turned off by high-pressured appeals for money.
- Because churches tend to be too one-sided politically (1986:22-25).

We could add other reasons, most notably the fact that many churches still deal with their members in the context of the nuclear family—which we know is only 7 percent of the population.

In fact, we could say that many churches have not recognized the changes and pressures facing our generation that I have covered throughout the pages of this book. If our needs aren't being met in one church, then we go somewhere else where they are.

Sims concludes his article with a helpful list of six points that churches should use in reaching and harnessing baby boomers.

- Recognize the difference between generations.
- Prepare to do things differently.
- Act on new ideas.
- Don't wait for the world to come to the church.
- Give women a meaningful way to be involved.
- Plan church activities realistically, taking into consideration lifestyles of the '80s and '90s (1986:25).

143

6. *Tread lightly with authority.* In my chapter "Coping with Career," I dealt with our generation's new views toward leadership and authority. This issue is very relevant in our churches, for the bottom line is that we resist heavy-handed leadership styles.

Leadership styles, like church methods for evangelism and edification, are methods that change through the generations. The Bible has much to say on the character of a good leader, and of the necessity of leadership, but little on styles that will work today. I believe in strong leadership, but I also believe in the concept of servant leadership. The two are not mutually exclusive.

An excellent book on this topic was written in the late '70s, a classic in the field of leadership, entitled *Servant Leadership* by Robert Greenleaf. I'll let him speak for our generation on this point, for he does a much better job than I could ever do:

"A fresh critical look is being taken at the issues of power and authority, and people are beginning to learn, however haltingly, to relate to one another in *less coercive and more creatively supporting ways*. A new moral principle is emerging which holds that the only authority deserving one's allegiance is that which is freely and knowingly granted by the led to the leader in response to, and in proportion to, *the clearly evident servant stature of the leader*. Those who choose to follow this principle will not casually accept the authority of existing institutions. *Rather, they will freely respond only to individuals who are chosen as leaders because they are proven and trusted as servants* (1977:9-10, emphasis added).

7. *Commit your church to excellence.* My personal observation is that many baby boomers who are committed to excellence in their work are turned off by the shabbiness that characterizes many local churches. They simply don't

feel comfortable in a dowdy-looking sanctuary with a low-tech sound system.

Baby boomers are used to up-scaled environments and high technology. When they walk into many churches, they simply feel like they are stepping into the past. It may be a wrong emphasis, but it is the way baby boomers feel. If we want to reach them, our appeal must be appetizing. This principle of excellence applies to both the appearance of the physical surroundings as well as to the effectiveness of the organization and administration of the programs of the church.

8. *For leaders from the older generation: welcome young, new leadership enthusiastically.* The 1990s will be a decade of transition. Churches and Christian organizations will be taken over by more and more baby boomers, if they haven't been already. We know that leadership transitions are not easy, but they must take place. In many cases there are young men and women moving into positions of leadership who have yet to receive the enthusiastic support of the older boards that oversee that work.

Boards of directors, or elder/deacon boards made up of older people in these churches and Christian organizations can cause a great deal of grief for the young boomers with a new generation of values and approaches. I admire the older leadership that says, "We've had our chance; now let's let them have a go of it." There comes a time in every generation when the torch must be passed from the older to the younger, and that time is now upon us.

9. *For leaders from the baby-boom generation: honor older leadership respectfully.* There is a critical balance here that must be maintained. It would be the ultimate mistake for baby boomers who come into leadership in our churches to write off the older generation and clean them off leadership teams. We must tap into their wisdom, yet help them gracefully let go of some of their traditions.

Baby boomers, beware. We must get past this immature

notion that everything old is bad and everything new is good. Worshiping change for change's sake is a shallow value that too many in our generation have adopted. No one wants to drive an old car or wear last year's fashions or use programs from a previous decade.

Old things can be beautiful and work better than newer innovations. Just look at the 1966 Ford Mustang, a beautiful car that was ruined as young designers kept trying to improve on something that should have been left alone. Now everyone wants a '66 Mustang!

Isn't it ironic that my generation hates tradition but loves antiques? There are traditions that are good, necessary, and completely functional in the 1990s and beyond. Let it not be said of our generation that we were too foolish to listen to the wisdom of our elders.

Baby boomers are having a great impact on churches, whether the churches like it or not. My prayer is that the churches of our land will have an even greater impact on the baby boomers, for there is much to harvest and much to harness among my peers for the cause of Christ.

References Cited

Anderson, Lisa
   1987   "Yuppies." *Chicago Tribune* September 30.

Barna Research Group
   1987   *Single Adults in America.* Glendale, Calif.: The
           Barna Research Group.

Bonhoeffer, Dietrich
   1959   *The Cost of Discipleship.* New York: Collier
           Books.

Bronstein, Phyllis and Carolyn Cowen, eds
   1988   *Fatherhood Today.* New York: John Wiley and
           Sons.

Burton, Linda, Janet Dittmer, Cheri Loveless
   1986   *What's a Smart Woman Like You Doing at
           Home?* Washington, D.C.: Acropolis Books.

Colsen, Charles
   1985   "A Call to Rescue the Yuppies." *Christianity To-
           day* May 17.

Dobson, James
   1987   *Love for a Lifetime.* Portland, Ore: Multnomah
           Press.

Finke, Nikki
1988 "Tweeners." *Los Angeles Times* January 24.

Forsman, Theresa
1987 "Making Way for the New Generation." *Hackensack, N.J. Record* April 12.

Goleman, Daniel
1986 "For Some Executives, Success Has a Terrible Price." *International Herald Tribune* August 25.

Gray, Charlotte
1983 "Baby Boom Women: High Hopes, Uncertain Prospects." *Chatelaine* August.

Greenleaf, Robert
1977 *Servant Leadership*. New York: Paulist Press.

Halvorsen, Karen
1987 "J.I. Packer Warns Against 'Yuppiedom.' " *Wheaton Alumni* August.

Hansel, Tim
1979 *When I Relax I Feel Guilty*. Elgin, Ill: David C. Cook.

Hersey, Paul and Ken Blanchard
1982 *Management of Organizational Behavior,* fourth edition. Englewood Cliffs, N.J.: Prentice Hall. (Table 3-1 based on original information in *The Human Side of Enterprise* by Douglas McGregor. Used by permission of McGraw Hill and Prentice Hall.)

Hershey, Terry
1984 *Intimacy*. Laguna Hills, Calif.: Merit Books.

Ingrassia, Michelle
1986 Series of Articles. *Newsday,* Long Island, N.Y. June 1-3.

Japenga, Ann
1988 "Dropping Back In." *Los Angeles Times* March 27.
Johnson, Otto, Executive Editor
1988 *The 1988 Information Please Almanac*. Boston: Houghton Mifflin.

Jones, Landon
1981 *Great Expectations: America and the Baby Boom Generation*. New York: Ballantine Books.

Krier, Beth Ann
1988 "Hanging On to the '60s." *Los Angeles Times* March 20.

Levine, Art
1986 "An Age of Remakes and Revivals." *U.S. News & World Report* November 24.

Makower, Joel
1985 *Boom! Talkin' about Our Generation*. Chicago: Contemporary Books.

Maynard, Rona
1984 "Are Baby Boom Mothers Pushing Their Kids Too Hard?" *Chatelaine* March.

McBee, Susan
1984 "Here Come the Baby Boomers." *U.S. News & World Report* November 4.

McGregor, Douglas
1960 *The Human Side of Enterprise*. New York: McGraw Hill.

Naisbitt, John
1984 *Megatrends*. New York: Warner Books.

Naisbitt, John and Patricia Aburdene
1985 *Re-Inventing the Corporation*. New York: Warner Books.

Niebuhr, Reinhold H.
1929   *The Social Sources of Denominationalism*. New York: World Publishing.

Rosellini, Lynn
1986   "You've Come a Long Way, Baby Boomers—When a Generation Turns Forty." *U.S. News & World Report* March 10.

Russell, Cheryl
1987   *100 Predictions for the Baby Boomer, The Next 50 Years*. New York: Plenum Press.

Sculley, John
1987   *Odyssey*. New York: Harper and Row. ("Contrasting Management Paradigms," p. 95 from *Odyssey* by John Sculley. © 1987 by John Scully. Reprinted by permission of Harper and Row Publishers, Inc.)

Simon, Roger
1988   "We Touch the Wall, and the Wall Touches Us." *TV Guide* May 28.

Sims, Jack
1986   "Baby Boomers: Time to Pass the Torch?" *Christian Life* January.

Talley, Jim and Bobbie Reed
1982   *Too Close, Too Soon*. Nashville: Thomas Nelson.

Thomas, Evan
1986   "Growing Pains at 40." *Time* May 19.

Toffler, Alvin
1980   *The Third Wave*. New York: Bantam Books.

1983   *Previews and Premises*. New York: William Morrow.

Trudeau, G.B.
1987   "Doonesbury." *L.A. Times* November 1 and *In-*

ternational Herald Tribune August 4.

Unger, Jim
   1987 "Herman" cartoon. *Los Angeles Times* November 1.

Whyte, William H.
   1956 *The Organization Man*. New York: Simon and Schuster.

Wiersbe, Warren
   1980 "Principles." *Leadership Journal.*

Worcester, John
   1987 *Reaching Baby Boomers*. Unpublished notes.

   1987 *Over the Hill Cards*, Anaheim, Calif.

   1984 "Baby Boomers Push for Power." *Businessweek* July 2.

248.84
F 516

92501

LINCOLN CHRISTIAN COLLEGE AND SEMINARY

3 4711 00092 9523